The Preacher'
Volume

Preaching from Hymns

John A Vickers

Other titles in the series

ISBN   1 85852 219 6

For the Revd G Thackray Eddy
and in memory of the
Revd George A E Cornforth
in belated acknowledgement
of a long-standing debt of gratitude

John Vickers began preaching as a VI-former, but decided that teaching rather than the pastoral ministry was his proper sphere. The last 14 years of his career were spent in teacher training. His books include a life of Dr Thomas Coke and the editing of two volumes on the 1851 Ecclesiastical Census, a volume of source material on British Methodism and *A Dictionary of Methodism in Britain and Ireland.* As the official indexer to the Wesley Works Project, he won the Wheatley Medal in 1977 for the index to the first volume in the new edition. He has served as British Secretary of the World Methodist Historical Society and has been involved for some years in Methodist historical publishing.

* * * * *

This book owes much to my friends the Revd Geoffrey R Senior and the Revd G Thackray Eddy, who have read and commented on it in draft form. Its blemishes and limitations, however, remain stubbornly my own.

John A Vickers

GENERAL
INTRODUCTION

Preaching is a very particular form of communication which has always been important in the life of the Christian Church. At the beginning of the 21st-century we are undergoing a revolution in the varieties, method and speed of our communications. Preachers of all denominations, ordained and lay, undertake this calling with an awareness that we preach in a changing context.

The Preacher's Library is designed to help us to think through, perhaps in some cases reassess, why we preach, how we preach, and to whom we preach. Some of the volumes in this series will take a fresh look at familiar issues, such as how preachers should approach various parts of the Bible, how we understand and express our doctrinal inheritance and the variety of styles in which preaching can be done. Other volumes will introduce issues which may be less familiar to many of us, such as the significance of our cultural context or the way in which the self-understanding of a woman preacher has important things to say to all preachers. Some of these books will offer direct help in the practice of preaching. Others will deal with issues which, although they appear more theoretical, impinge upon the preacher's task and on which we therefore need to have reflected if we are to preach with integrity in today's world.

All the writers in this series, lay and ordained, women and men, are recognised preachers within their own denominations and write with the needs of their colleagues firmly in mind. These books will avoid academic jargon, but they will not avoid dealing with difficult issues. They are offered to other preachers in the belief that as we deepen our thinking and hone our skills

God's people will be blessed and built up to the glory of God.

Research regularly shows that hymns are a greatly valued part of worship for most churchgoers, and that even amongst non-churchgoers they constitute part of folk-religion. But what are hymns for, and do we think about the words we sing? An important book on 18th-century hymnody, published some 20 years ago, concluded that whereas the hymns of writers such as Isaac Watts aimed to help worshippers express their devotional states, those of the Wesley brothers aimed to teach people to feel religiously. Dr Vickers clearly believes that good hymns teach us to feel religiously, that is, to enter into the experience about which we sing and find ourselves changed by it. This being the case, there is a rich material in hymns for the preacher to use, not as an alternative to scripture, but as a means of enabling the congregation to share in the experience of God's grace to which scripture bears witness. Of course, if we are to preach from hymns we shall want to subject them to rigorous critical scrutiny, and Dr Vickers does not hesitate to do that.

This book will teach preachers to look with new eyes at the hymns they choose and will challenge them to use those hymns in new ways. Congregations, in turn, will learn again how the hymns they love to sing can become means by which the Christian faith is made real to them.

Michael J Townsend

CONTENTS

1

HYMNS AND THE PREACHER

One thing to be made clear at the outset is that this is not another book on 'how to preach'. That must be left to the expert practitioners, the James Stewarts, Will Sangsters and Colin Morrises, who have sound credentials for offering such advice. After half a century of experience in the pulpit, I have no illusions of belonging to their company. What I have attempted here is to consider just one among several aspects of *preparing* to preach. In my own experience the hymn book is a treasure store, not just of Christian devotional writing, but of material that can inform and enrich the sermons we prepare. It does not, of course, stand alone in that respect, but alongside great literature, and especially poetry (though we no longer quote Browning and the other poets as freely as our Victorian predecessors did!), alongside our own experience of life and that of others known to us, and, of course, the Bible above all. Although biblical exposition is one of several topics that crop up only incidentally in this book, it will be clear enough, I hope, that I am nowhere commending the hymn book as an alternative or rival to Scripture, but rather (to use the quaint language of the past) as its handmaid. Similarly, although it would obviously be impossible to write about preaching without reference to Christian doctrine, I do so by way of illustration only; for expert guidance on theology, you must look elsewhere than to a Church historian. If any of my examples provoke you to protest or to counterargument, so much the better. A book is not worth reading if it does not drive you to think for yourself.

Hymns and their authors can, of course, serve as sermon illustrations. But here the historian in me kicks in, to warn you that some of the most frequently repeated stories are apocryphal. Despite the plaque you will find in Burrington Combe, it is at least doubtful whether Toplady wrote 'Rock of Ages' (*HP* 273) while sheltering there from a thunderstorm; while that favourite children's address about how James T East wrote 'Wise men seeking Jesus' (*HP* 128) after forgoing a visit to the Holy Land was dismissed by the author's own daughter as a fable.

If I were taking a text to serve as my starting point, it would probably be from chapter 23 of Thomas Love Peacock's *Gryll Grange*, where Mr Macborrowdale observes to the Revd Dr Opimian, 'I am afraid, doctor, if you look for profound knowledge in popular poetry, you will often be disappointed.' To which the doctor replies, 'I do not look for profound knowledge. But I do expect that poets should understand what they talk of.' Change that last sentence so that it speaks of worshippers understanding what they sing of and you have the underlying assumption of all that follows. In other words, my focus throughout is on the *meaning* of the hymns we sing, i.e. on the way they express or reflect what we believe, rather than on their literary or other qualities. Other aspects of hymnology have been effectively dealt with in other books (some of which are mentioned in the reading list at the end), but I have not encountered one which tackles their use in sermon preparation in any detail. In any case, the range of hymns we have at our disposal is constantly changing, as I have tried to reflect in what follows.

Dr Philip Watson, a leading 20th-century authority on the theology of Martin Luther, would never sing the line 'Through faithful service cometh full salvation' (*HP* 798 v.3). In retrospect, I have to conclude that he knew Luther's doctrine of salvation by faith alone better than he knew John Wesley's concern for 'scriptural holiness' as part of our salvation. Wesley's threefold emphasis was on repentance, faith and holiness: 'the first . . . we account, as it were, the porch of religion, the next the door, the third, religion itself'. (Elsewhere he speaks of 'faith, holiness and good works, as the root, the tree and the fruit which God has joined and man ought not to put asunder'.) Whether you side with Luther or Wesley in this matter, Watson's example is one worth following. If there are lines, or even whole hymns, which we find we cannot conscientiously join in singing, that is at least a sign that we are thinking about the meaning of the words. It is surely reasonable to encourage the same among our congregations?

Let us be clear from the outset, however, that hymns are more than just doctrinal statements. To be worth singing, a hymn does not necessarily have to provide 'food for thought'; it may do no more than express a mood, whether penitence, anxiety, confidence or joy, or indeed aspiration towards some unattainable goal such as the 'perfect love' (or Christian perfection) on which the Wesleys so insisted. A hymn such as 'When Easter to the dark world came' (*HP* 200) does little more than enumerate events from the first Easter (hoping that, even in these biblically illiterate days, we will be able to fill in the details for ourselves); but aided as much by its jaunty tune as by the words, it effectively expresses for us the joyful mood of Easter morning. All the same, we need a more varied and nourishing diet than this if we are to stay spiritually healthy and to grow in grace.

John Betjeman writes in *Summoned by Bells* of being 'safe in the surge of undogmatic hymns'. But it is difficult, if not impossible, for even the simplest of hymns to be devoid of any doctrinal content, and if our understanding of the faith we profess is influenced, however unconsciously, by what we habitually sing, then it is important that we, as worshippers, give some attention to its meaning, in order to sing meaningfully. If we think we can safely switch off our minds when we come to worship and rely entirely on an emotional autopilot, we had better think again – or begin thinking for the first time. When an

engineer or scientist or administrator or teacher does not
see the need to match his professional skills with her
worshipping skills, something has gone wrong (and not
merely with the syntax of this politically correct sentence!).

That does not mean that we have to be high-calibre
intellectuals before we can offer worship worthy of the
one who exhorted us to love God with all our *minds* (Mark
12:30 etc.); but merely that we should be using such
intelligence as we have been endowed with if we are to
honour our creator. For this reason I am uneasy with a
statement like 'Faith believes, *nor questions how*' (*HP* 592
v.2). That human reason has its limitations, however
prone we may be to forget them in this 'modern' age, is a
simple fact of experience for even the most highly
intelligent. But that it can therefore be safely discarded is
a view better left to the postmodernists: 'blind faith' is not
to be commended. As Father Brown insisted in his
conversation with the celebrated criminal Flambeau on
Hampstead Heath, it is always bad theology to attack
reason. The proper relationship between reason and faith
is expressed by Isaac Watts:

> Where reason fails with all her powers,
> There faith prevails, and love adores. (*HP* 18 v.4)

When we *have* exhausted reason's powers, then in the
humility of believing we can rightly pray for

> Faith to wrestle with the mystery
> Of a God who loves and cares. (*HP* 75 v.2)

More frequently than we perhaps are conscious of, the
words we sing express an ideal rather than the reality of
life as it is, and there is no harm in that, provided we
recognise the difference and are prepared to renew our
striving towards the ideal being expressed – or remain
silent. The image of a world 'weary . . . of selfish greed
and fruitless pain . . . and all its ancient deeds of wrong' in
HP 399 v.3 could hardly be much further from the world
we live in; otherwise there would be much greater hope
for its future than appears at present. Some 19th-century
hymns speak of the Church in terms that are very far

removed from the Church as we know it; e.g. 'City of God, how broad and far . . .' (*HP* 809) or 'The church's one foundation' (*HP* 515). Similarly, Charles Wesley's 'See how great a flame aspires . . .' (*HP* 781) paints a picture that is only remotely like the rise of Methodism seen through the eyes of an impartial historian. Again, the same writer's treatment of the Incarnation in v.2 of *HP* 400, 'All glory to God in the sky', is wildly idealistic from a historical point of view. But only someone who 'hath no music in himself, nor is not mov'd with concord of sweet sounds' would take this as a reason for not singing these hymns. The proviso mentioned above still applies, however, and not least in a more personal context, as when we sing

> Take my silver and my gold,
> Not a mite would I withhold. (*HP* 705 v.4)

I have heard it argued, with some justification, that few if any of us have a right to use such words in the presence of the God who knows us better than we know ourselves. But as a sincere aspiration, and a challenge to be faced, it may have an important place in our devotion.

The treasury of Christian hymnology is part of the joint stock of the whole Church of God and there are no denominational barriers or frontiers to limit our inheritance. For practical reasons, as well as because of the limits of my own acquaintance with that treasure, most of the hymns referred to here will be found in *Hymns & Psalms* (1983), with occasional reference to its predecessor, the *Methodist Hymn Book* of 1933 (referred to as *HP* and *MHB* respectively). Despite this, many, perhaps most, of the examples I have taken will be found in other denominational collections, and it is my hope that what I have written may prove of wider interest and use to preachers. In any case, whatever your denominational background, the book should be read with a hymn book open at its side.

2

WORSHIP

Hymns have become a virtually universal feature of public worship, and though the collections we use are mostly denominational in origin, their interdenominational contents do more to bridge the gaps between our still separated traditions than any other feature of our 'ecumenical' age. More remarkable than we often pause to realise is the fact that, whatever our own allegiance, we find ourselves comfortable with hymns by Roman Catholics, Orthodox and Protestants (whether Lutheran, Presbyterian or Anglican), or with both the uncompromisingly Arminian Charles Wesley and the Calvinistic Augustus Montague Toplady, whose criticism of the Wesleys led him into downright scurrility. This catholicity is certainly true at the 'grass-roots' level where most of us operate. Another way in which hymns enrich worship is by linking us to past generations of Christian worshippers and, increasingly, to fellow Christians around the world. Twenty centuries of devotion and praise have gone into the making of any hymn book worthy of serious consideration. The hymn-writing tradition is undoubtedly alive and well, but to sing nothing except what has been written in the past generation or so is to be inevitably impoverished.

That what is sometimes dismissed as a 'hymn sandwich' should be considered less acceptable than a 'prayer sandwich' is something that has long intrigued me. It should not be necessary at this late date to argue the case for hymns as part of public worship; only for taking them seriously and singing them thoughtfully. But some denominations were much more hesitant than others in 'taking hymn-singing into their system'. It is remarkable to find Archbishop Benson, as late as 1890, declaring that hymns might be allowed in public worship 'provided they did not interrupt the course of the service'. Such a view perhaps lingers on in the custom of the 'offertory hymn' during which the collection plate is passed round: a practice that I can only describe as liturgical slovenliness, debasing both the hymn-singing and the offertory.

But do we often enough consider what it is we are doing (or claiming to do) when we gather for worship? It is surely our responsibility as preachers to see that our congregations do so from time to time, rather than participating merely out of habit or inclination.

In *HP* 792 , Horatius Bonar's 'Fill thou my life, O Lord my God', v.2 offers a simple analysis of the way in which we are called to praise God – with voice, heart and life. *HP* 484, 'Angel voices, ever singing', provides a variety of thoughts about worship, including the initial reminder that ours is only a small part of the whole, which is not confined even to this planet. It should be a source of unending wonder and adoration that God should take account of, and even delight in, our human worship (v.2). So we can confidently bring him the offering of all the talents and skills we have been endowed with (vv3 and 4). But only our best is good enough (v.5). Here is a challenging yardstick by which to measure our offering of praise. If we were to take it to heart, I suspect that we might have second thoughts about some of the antics we adopt in our efforts to be up-to-date.

But the externals of worship are a secondary consideration, to be evaluated in terms of how far they contribute to its essential purpose. Isaac Watts in *HP* 297 gets far closer to the heart of the matter. The real danger is that of lapsing into mere formality through worship becoming a matter of habit, rather than the most presumptuous activity of all. Worship is our response in a conversation which is always initiated by God. Since 'we love because he first loved us' (1 John 4:10, 19), we need to pray at the outset of every act of devotion, corporate or individual,

> Come, shed abroad the Saviour's love,
> And that shall kindle ours. (v.4)

We can only rise to the occasion if God himself, the Holy Spirit, inspires and enables us, as *HP* 304 reminds us in simple but effective language and as Paul insists in Romans 8:26-27.

Whether our chosen mode is exuberant and extrovert or restrained and traditional, one essential ingredient is surely a sense of awe and unworthiness in the presence of the Holy One who is the source of all existence. Many hymns express this for us, none more briefly and effectively than Charles Wesley's line, 'The wonder – Why such love to me?' (*MHB* 325 v.4), which we have now lost, together with the lines which speak of

> The speechless awe that dares not move,
> And all the silent heaven of love. (v.5)

Fortunately, the temple robbers have still left us Isaac Watts' 'Eternal Power, whose high abode' (*HP* 49), with its closing reminder that silence can sometimes be more eloquent than words:

> A sacred reverence checks our songs,
> And praise sits silent on our tongues.

Such speechlessness expresses a sense of God as ineffable, as recognised in *HP* 7, 8, 9, 12 and many other hymns of praise.

The obverse of this is a sense of our utter unworthiness of God's love. It is a commonplace of our human relationships that love can never be bought, or earned, or deserved. How much more true must it be of our relationship with God. This is recognised in a number of hymns and pervades many others, from George Herbert's version of the 23rd Psalm:

> ... And all this not for my desert,
> But for his holy name (*HP* 43 v.3)

to Robert Bridges'

> Therefore, kind Jesus, since I cannot pay thee,
> I do adore thee, and will ever pray thee,
> Think on thy pity and thy love unswerving,
> Not my deserving (*HP* 164 v.5)

and Tilak's

> One who is all unfit to count
> As scholar in thy school ... (*HP* 539)

It is also, in more diffused form, the theme of the hymn Charles Wesley wrote following his 'conversion', 'And can it be . . .' (*HP* 216), though the inappropriate robustness of the eminently singable 'Sagina' to which the hymn is set, serves to highlight its other theme of confidence in God's love. (It would help if we were able to bring ourselves to sing the hymn to the tune 'Abingdon' (*HP* 500) which Erik Routley wrote as an alternative to 'Sagina'.) Without a prior sense of our unworthiness that love ceases to inspire a due sense of wonder and thankfulness.

Finally, an apparent contrast between

> Take my love; my Lord, I pour
> At thy feet its treasure-store. (*HP* 705 v.6)

and

> What shall we offer our good Lord,
> Poor nothings, for his boundless grace? (*HP* 807 v.1)

('Poor nothings' refers to *us* in comparison with the Almighty, though by a slight change in the punctuation it can be made to refer to our offerings – as I suspect it is more often than not understood, because the tune 'Duke Street' nudges us in that direction.)

Which of these two couplets is nearer the truth? Are they contradictory, or are they expressing complementary facets of the truth? Is the love we feel towards God a 'treasure store'; or are we (or our offerings) 'poor nothings'? Consideration of such questions should make us and our congregations understand more fully the significance of the activity we call 'worship'.

Fred Pratt Green has given us a delightful hymn on the role of music in worship (*HP* 388). But I would happily sacrifice that to reclaim one whose absence from *Hymns & Psalms* I regret. This is his 'When the Church of Jesus/Shuts its outer door', which appeared as no. 74 in *Hymns & Songs* (1969). It reminds us that, in drawing aside to worship God, we should not turn our backs on the world he has made and put us in. There is some compensation for this loss in a single line from *HP* 401: 'Let not our worship blind us to the claims of love' (v.4), a text that cries out to be expounded, with a reference perhaps to Leigh Hunt's poem about Abou Ben Adhem.

3

ALTERATIONS

In his Preface to the *Collection of Hymns for the Use of the People Called Methodists* (1780) John Wesley made a well-known plea that anyone who used his or his brother's hymns should do so without altering them. 'I desire they would not attempt to mend them – for really they are not able.' So, if anyone *did* use them, he begged them 'to let them stand just as they are, to take them for better, for worse'.

Despite this, the fact is that Wesley was himself quite capable of adapting other writers' hymns to his own purpose or taste. Witness what he did to some of George Herbert's verses, to make them, as he saw it, suitable for congregational use, as when he 'improved' that exquisite hymn of praise 'King of Glory, King of peace' (*HP* 499)to make it, as he saw, suitable for congregational use and made it into:

O King of glory, King of peace,
  Thee only will I love;
Thee, that my love may never cease,
  Incessant will I move.

And so on through the rest of the hymn in similar clodhopping vein. Nor did Wesley heed his own advice in making editorial emendations to his brother Charles' hymns. But this is hardly surprising. In pleading for no alterations, Wesley was in fact emulating Canute's attempt to control the tide, since, quite apart from the vagaries of translation into other languages, hymns have always been fair game for would-be 'improvers'. And it is only fair to add that editing and rewriting has sometimes enabled a hymn to survive the theological and cultural changes and so continue 'to serve the present age'.

One indication of honest editing is that compilers of a new hymn book should show when changes of any substance have been made to the text of a hymn. But anyone familiar with the 1933 *Methodist Hymn Book* or its predecessors will readily spot such changes, without looking for the tell-tale 'alt.' at the end. More to our present purpose, changes that have seemed necessary or desirable can provide food for thought, and therefore may become the starting point for sermon-making. Here are a few examples.

To begin with a well known hymn in which the changes are both extensive and significant. 'Hills of the North, rejoice' (*MHB* 815) enjoyed great popularity in the heyday of overseas missions. Its extensive rewriting as *HP* 237 reflects the fundamental changes in both the circumstances and the theology of mission that took place in the later 20th century. Here is plenty of material for a sermon on the World Church of our own time, not to mention changing attitudes towards other world faiths.

We may note, at the outset, that the hymn has been moved from 'Missions at Home and Abroad' to a section of the new book on 'Christ's Coming in Glory'. This represents a significant shift of emphasis – from the missionary Church to Christ himself as the Saviour of the world and his final triumph – which could be explored in a sermon on what has been called 'the latent Christ'. Where the original hymn might be said to be dismissive, or at best patronising, in its assumption that Christianity had a monopoly of saving truth, now phrase after phrase assumes Christ at work in the world beyond the bounds of Christendom. He is the one who 'comes in righteousness and love', in whom all 'shall be made anew'. Most significant are the phrases which assume Christ's unrecognised presence in what was once dismissed as the 'heathen' world. The 'lands of the east' whose hills had formerly been 'long cold and grey' and which were exhorted to wake up to realise their freedom in Christ, now are invited to recognise him as not their first but their *'brightest* morn' (i.e. there have been others before this, but none so bright), the 'final [but not the 'first'] Word', and one whom their seers have longed to know. In other words the 'darkest night' over which Christ has triumphed is *'ours'*, not just theirs, so that

> In Jesus *all* shall find their rest,
> In him *the universe* be blest.

Does this offer an opportunity to invite a fresh look at John 14:6, a verse which for many has been a stumbling-block in the way of doing justice to what is good and true in other world religions and recognising a God who has been, not selectively, but universally at work in human history and culture (as hinted at by Peter in Acts 10:34-35 and by Paul in Acts 17:22-23)? Unless we are prepared to retreat into the ghetto mentality of belief in a God to whom the majority of the human race seems to be of no concern, here is a growing point in our understanding of his activity in the world.

Less conspicuously, but quite unambiguously, v.5 of *HP* 783 has been changed to take account of this new recognition of God's presence and activity in the world as a whole, beyond the confines of his Church. The 'heathen lands afar' of *MHB* 811 have become 'lands both near and far' – a recognition of the fact that mission begins at home, wherever that may be. Similarly, there is James Montgomery's stirring (if triumphalist) hymn, 'Lift up your heads, ye gates of brass' (*HP* 227), where in v.5 the line 'To him shall all the nations bow' has replaced the original 'To Christ shall Buddha's votaries bow'. The change speaks for itself, but again, could be made the starting point for a sermon on Christianity and other world faiths. Furthermore, the restoration of v.2, which was not included in *MHB* 265, invites one to consider what Montgomery meant by the phrase *'mysteriously* at strife'

13

and what (if anything) he may have had in mind when he wrote of engaging 'for more than death or life'.

A more recent hymn which offers a number of opportunities to explore this theme is *HP* 412, which is addressed to the 'God of every nation'. Fred Kaan reveals something of what he means by that phrase in the rest of the hymn; notably in

Your love is at the heart of all creation (v.1)

and

Speak to the soul of all the human race. (v.3)

Elsewhere in the hymn, these generalisations are interpreted in more concrete terms, bringing down to earth what might otherwise remain no more that bland, if unexceptional, sentiments. And if you are looking for a text which might serve to launch a sermon on the topic, try *HP* 324 v.3:

His the truth behind the wisdoms
Which as yet know not our Lord;

It is tempting to add to this Faber's well known stanza:

For the love of God is broader
Than the measures of man's mind;
And the heart of the Eternal
Is most wonderfully kind. (*HP* 230 v.4)

The principle is undoubtedly there in embryo, but I am less sure that Faber was embracing other religious traditions: more likely, he had got only as far as recognising Protestant Christians as equally the object of God's love. That in itself was a remarkable anticipation of the ecumenical movement by one who had followed Newman into the Roman Church. Today we have to reckon with the possibility that the principle may have even wider implications than Faber realised.

* * * * *

In pursuing this theme, we have got away from significant alterations and it is time to return to them. Charles Wesley's hymn, 'A charge to keep I have' (*MHB* 578) focuses on a more personal issue and has survived into *Hymns & Psalms* as no. 785, but with a significant change to its closing lines.

> Assured, if I my trust betray,
> I shall for ever die.

has become

> So shall I not my trust betray,
> Nor love within me die.

The alteration raises the question of our final or eternal destiny. We no longer hear warnings of hell-fire from our pulpits; indeed, when did you last either hear or preach a sermon on any aspect of life after death? But it is as well to remember that the question of whether the punishment of the wicked was 'everlasting' or only for a certain period was one which still exercised the minds and hearts of Christian thinkers well into the 20th century. Those who dared to question the justice (or even the mercy) of a God who consigned a majority of the human race to an eternity of hell-fire were condemned and even cast out as dangerous heretics.

Charles Wesley's words at the end of this hymn are mild and merciful by comparison with such fierce orthodoxy. The worst fate he contemplates for those who fail the test is that they will 'for ever die'. That punishment is, at least, a negative one, the loss of the bliss of eternal life in the presence of their Creator. But even that, it seems, was too strong a concept for the editors of *Hymns & Psalms* and we may rejoice that they have here redefined hell as a failure to love in response to the 'love that will not let me go'. This is very much in line with Charles Wesley's reiteration of the theme that 'heaven is love' (and is therefore anticipated, at least in part, in our earthly experience).

There would be widespread agreement, I think, that 'When I survey the wondrous cross' (*HP* 180) is Isaac Watts' greatest hymn. It is certainly one of the towering peaks in the range and far from being merely a foothill of English hymn-writing. For a full exploration of its literary and spiritual qualities, see Richard Watson's profound analysis in his *The English Hymn* pp161-70. It is also worth noting the similarities, as well as the very real differences, between it and *HP* 181, 'Were you there when they crucified my Lord?' Here I shall merely pick up one or two quite simple details from Watts' hymn. It is interesting to note that in the earliest version Watts wrote of 'the *young* Prince of Glory', but changed the line himself to the form we are more familiar with. To construct a sermon on that one adjective would, no doubt, be to risk being trite or banal: 'Here we have the supreme illustration of the fact that a life is not to be measured by longevity, but by the quality and significance of what is achieved.' If that is all the truth we want to convey, we might do better to take a lesser example, such as Mozart! But it is just conceivable that the thought of 'the young Prince of Glory' cut off in his prime might serve as a peg on which to hang a consideration of our Lord's utter humanity: the paradox of 'the Immortal dies' which is at the heart of God's self-revelation in Christ.

The compilers of *Hymns & Psalms* have given us back v.4, missing for many years from the *Methodist Hymn Book*. Whether it improves the hymn is perhaps debatable. The simile in line 1 may strike us today as more repulsive than it did to Watts' contemporaries. Watts is versifying Paul's words in Galatians 6:14, but, perhaps under the constraint of needing a rhyme, writes of being dead, not to 'the world', but to 'the globe'. I find myself torn in opposite directions here. On the one hand, now that we have seen pictures of our planet beamed back from space the word 'globe' has been enriched for us. But it is surely more significant to note that being 'dead to the world' is more meaningful than being 'dead to our physical environment'. The world Paul calls us to be 'crucified unto' is the environment of sin, of self-centredness and pride and of wilful defiance of God's purposes – which certainly has consequences for our physical environment, but goes very much deeper than that. In an age when this-worldliness penetrates deeply into our Western way of life, affecting Christians and 'unbelievers' alike, we can surely not afford to lose any shades of meaning in what Paul is saying here.

There is a word in v.5 which, if we were brought up on the *Methodist Hymn Book*, is likely to give us pause. The compilers have given us back Watts' own word here, 'present', in place of the 'offering' substituted by others. Am I the only one to whom 'present' seems inadequate, conveying a sense of the commonplace, whereas 'offering' adds considerable weight to the meaning? Richard Watson argues for the opposite view: that 'present' is part of the 'controlled, unemotional' vocabulary which is an important part of the hymn's success. I, on the other hand, am reminded of the banality into which Wordsworth sometimes stumbled when he applied his own principle of preferring the language of everyday speech to the artificial vocabulary and style of contemporary poetry. A 'present' is something relatively trivial (apart from the 'thought behind it'), something a little less than a 'gift', perhaps, in common parlance, and certainly without the overtones of an 'offering' (which may vary according to the context from an artistic offering to the sacrificial). Here, at least, we might help a congregation to explore the nature and quality of our response to God's unique offering of himself in Christ.

Finally, if you are looking for an alteration on which to exercise your puzzle-solving ability, try *HP* 637 v.2 line 2, where 'The world, it is Thy word' (*MHB* 930) has become 'Earth is thy uttered word'. This is not a case of reverting to the author's original words, since what George MacDonald actually wrote was 'The world is all a sign'. Any explanation for the changes must take into account whatever distinction may be made between 'the world' and 'the earth', and also the significance of the adjective 'uttered'. I've thought of four or five possible, but not very convincing, explanations so far; how about you?

4

SERMON OUTLINES

O ne of the most obvious ways in which hymns may support or inform our preaching is by providing ready-made outlines for a sermon. Some hymns are particularly obvious examples of this, since they have a clearly discernible structure which may readily become the outline of a sermon. Several of the hymns on, or to, the Holy Spirit, for example, have such a structure; but these will be dealt with at a later stage.

Oliver Beckerlegge, in the Introduction to the new edition of Wesley's 1780 *Collection of Hymns,* draws attention to the way in which Charles Wesley uses the unusual stanza form '6 6.7.7.7.7.' as a kind of mini-sermon. The first two lines, he says, announce the text which is then expounded in the remainder of the verse. His example is *MHB* 97, 'O filial Deity', which you will not find in *Hymns & Psalms;* but his point is illustrated by *HP* 541, especially vv1 and 3. No other examples have survived in present-day use, however.

HP 552, 'Lord of all hopefulness', is a convenient example of a hymn offering a useful outline. It has a simple, and indeed obvious, progression through the hours of the day. But there is more to be found beneath the surface and a congregation might well be helped to explore the hymn at greater depth. Parallel with and enriching the significance of its progression from dawn through noon and evening to bedtime are two parallel sequences: one in which Christ is presented as Lord of hopefulness and joy, of eagerness and faith, of kindliness and grace, and of gentleness and calm, and the other in which we ask for the equivalent gifts of bliss, strength, love and peace. The hymn's effectiveness lies very much in the way in which these three strands are woven together, but also in the closeness of the ideas to our own everyday experience and needs. The underlying theme is, of course, that of the realised presence of Christ at all times in our daily life; so that the hymn is, in effect, a contemporary application of Brother Lawrence's *Practice of the Presence of God* in and through whatever mundane activities engage our minds and hands. For most of us it is surely true that, if we do not find God at the kitchen sink, in the study or the workshop, we are not likely to find him anywhere. So, whether or not I follow the fourfold outline provided by this hymn, its underlying theme provides a useful starting-point for a sermon that should prove meaningful to most congregations.

One of Fred Pratt Green's most popular hymns, *HP* 455, provides the outline for a sermon on Christ as the world's Light, Peace and Life, reaching its climax in a final doxology. And in *HP* 709 Timothy Dudley-Smith writes of Christ in an ascending scale as leader, teacher and Saviour. It is not difficult to see how either of these outlines could be filled out. And another modern hymn that would readily lend itself to being turned into a four-part sermon is Caryl Micklem's 'Give to me, Lord, a thankful heart' (*HP* 548).

HP 675, 'Have faith in God, my heart', by Bryn Rees has a simple three-verse structure (heart, mind and soul), summed up in the final verse's prayer, 'Lord Jesus, make me *whole* . . .' The concluding reference to being made 'the captive of your grace' would in itself serve as a meaningful text for any preacher willing to explore its implications and might well evoke a reference to George Matheson's paradoxical 'Make me a captive, Lord,/And then I shall be free' (*HP* 714). Another of Rees' hymns, *HP* 139, challenges us with a more complex pattern of thought. It has secured its place in contemporary worship; partly, no doubt, because its robust wording is set to a good, singable tune, but also because it challenges us to think about the meaning of the 'kingdom of God'. Its structure is most explicit in the second line of each verse, where the various definitions of what the kingdom is are reinforced by the alliteration: 'justice and joy', 'challenge and choice', 'the gift and the goal'. But exactly here arises the, for me, inescapable query, even as I sing the words: 'What, then, about "mercy and grace" in v.2?' Is the absence of alliteration here merely a literary failure? 'Goodness and grace' would certainly sacrifice some of the meaning of the more specific 'mercy and grace' and so the latter can readily be justified. If so, then we are encouraged to look for meaning, and not just rhetorical facility, in the couplings in the other verses; and these might well be explored with a congregation.

I find that I have to dig quite deep to find the connection between 'justice' and 'joy' in v.1; but that in itself is no bad thing. In v.2 the coupling of 'mercy' and 'grace' sends me back to an older hymn, 'Rock of Ages' (*HP* 273), which speaks of Christ's blood as 'the *double* cure' of sin, cleansing us from 'its *guilt* and *power*'. In other words, reverting to Bryn Rees' words, God's grace takes us a significant step beyond his mercy: forgiveness is not an end in itself, but leads to restoration and commitment. In v.3 the 'challenge' and 'choice' are two sides of a single coin, the divine and the human; and in v.4 we are reminded that in Christ's teaching the kingdom is spoken of as both present *and* future, as a gift we can receive here and now, but also a future goal, not only of individual endeavour, but of human history. Here is wealth indeed, perhaps far more than a single sermon can encompass!

HP 172, 'O dearest Lord, thy sacred head', could clearly be used as an outline for a sermon on serving God with our minds, in our activities, in our obedience or response to circumstances, and, above all, with our innermost being. *HP* 413, 'We pray for peace', invites us to think of different kinds of peace, including dubious or spurious ones. And in *HP* 685 George Matheson characterises Christ as love, light and joy, bringing his hymn to a climax in a response to the cross which supremely reveals the 'love that will not let us go'. (Was Francis Thompson familiar with Matheson's hymn when he wrote so powerfully of the relentless pursuit of 'the Hound of Heaven'? The poem could certainly be quoted to great effect in any sermon on this theme.)

HP 238 with its repeated 'I cannot tell . . .', meaning not just 'I cannot describe or explain', but 'I cannot comprehend . . .', is an invitation to explore Christian agnosticism in its deepest, truest sense. We have to learn to live with unanswered, perhaps unanswerable, questions about the Incarnation (v.1), Christ's Passion (v.2) and the future (vv3 and 4). But beyond the horizons of our knowledge lie momentous certainties.

HP 532, 'Lord Christ, we praise your sacrifice', perhaps provides the basis for a series of sermons, rather than a single over-packed one. Look at the closing couplet of each verse and note how in each case Alan Gaunt uses a paradox to drive home its meaning. 'Power and weakness', 'Victory through defeat', 'Life and hope through death': themes woven together in the closing verse, with its challenge to us to 'give our lives away and claim [our] victory today'.

On the other hand, we do not need a whole hymn to provide us with a sermon outline. There are many single verses, couplets or even single lines which will suffice; e.g.. *HP* 62 v.1:

> Our strength, thy grace; our rule, thy word;
> Our end, the glory of the Lord

the perfect framework for a three-part sermon.

Charles Wesley, in particular, has the ability to put so much meaning into a single line that one sermon may seem hardly enough to unpack it. Take, for instance, the tremendous line in verse 2 of *HP* 520 ('Father, whose everlasting love'), where God's 'everlasting love' is described as 'immense, unfathomed, unconfined'. In a lesser writer, we might suspect to find the trio of adjectives to be tautologous, but with Wesley we may confidently look for distinctions and shades of meaning. God's love is 'immense'; so far so good – it is *his* love, the real thing, not our weak human reflection of it, that we are concerned with. From this initial consideration, we are invited to go on to the thought that it is a love too vast or deep to be measured or comprehended by our finite minds. And finally, perhaps the most fundamental conviction in Wesley's theology: that this love is all-embracing, 'So wide, it never passed by one, or it had passed by *me*.'

Here are a few others from *Hymns & Psalms* for you to consider:

Whole verses:

340 v.6: John Keble on the blinding influence of the prevailing materialistic culture, even (or especially?) on Christians:

> Two worlds are ours; 'tis only sin
> Forbids us to descry
> The mystic heaven and earth within,
> Plain as the sea and sky.

341 v.2, in which Percy Dearmer provides a basis for a sermon on the need for a distinctive Christian lifestyle:

> Give pure happiness in leisure,
> Temperance in every pleasure,
> Wholesome use of earthly treasure,
> Bodies clear and spirits bright.

354 v.5, a call to faithful discipleship; a mosaic of biblical allusions, especially from Jesus' parables and Paul's words in 2 Timothy 4:7:

> O that each in the day
> Of his coming may say:
> 'I have fought my way through,
> I have finished the work thou didst give me to do!'

500 v.5 provides an opportunity to explore the nature of Christian liberty, an updating, if you like, of one of Martin Luther's favourite themes:

> Lord God, in Christ you set us free
> Your life to live, your joy to share . . .

This is also the theme of 534 v.4, though without the sharply focused detail of Brian Wren's verse and with a hint of sentimentality that is only partly redeemed by the use of paradox:

> Lord, it is coming to ourselves
> When thus we come to thee;
> The bondage of thy loveliness
> Is perfect liberty.

Though *HP* 739 was apparently written for children, there is plenty in v.1 to serve as material for a sermon on daily discipleship:

> May the mind of Christ my Saviour
> Live in me from day to day,
> By his love and power controlling
> All I do or say.

The first line, of course, echoes Philippians 2:5, a passage which gives content to the phrase 'the mind of Christ'. The phrase 'day to day' and the conjunction of 'love and power' (motivation and strength?) suggest other sub-headings. Finally, though the word 'controlling' may suggest that Christ 'takes over' and deprives his followers of responsibility for their own lives, experience teaches us differently. However much his influence may pervade our daily life, he never usurps our freedom of choice, but enters into partnership with us.

Fred Pratt Green's hymns always provide rich 'food for thought', and in the opening verse of *HP* 804, 'The Church of Christ, in every age,' he comes near to Charles Wesley in packing meaning into a single line, describing the Church as 'beset by change but Spirit-led'. Tease out the implications of those few words and you have a challenging sermon on the calling and mission of today's Church. Or you might start from v.5, which sums up the rest of the hymn.

Couplets:

75 v.1:   where Christ is described as being

> Crowned in deep humiliation
> By your partners in God's plan.

142 v.4:   And they who fain would serve thee best
> Are conscious most of wrong within.

168 v.5:   Filled with joy, and love, and peace,
> Perfected in holiness.

209 v.4:   To them the cross, with all its shame,
> With all its grace, is given.

226 v.6:   O unexampled love,
> O all-redeeming grace!

275 v.2:   To me, with thy dear name, are given
> Pardon, and holiness, and heaven.

395 v.3:   Release in us those healing truths
> Unconscious pride resists or shelves.

425 v.3:   What skill and science slowly gain
> Is soon to evil ends betrayed.
(But this needs to be balanced by the concluding verse of the hymn!)

464 v.5:   Walk in the light: and thine shall be
> No thornless path, but bright.

499 v.3:   In my heart, though not in heaven,
> I can raise thee.

544 v.4:   To feel thy power, to hear thy voice,
> To know thy love, be all my choice.

556 v.1: But how much more than us they have to give,
            Who by their dying show us how to live!

564 v.3: I thank thee too that often joy
            Is touched with pain.
(But what about 'pain touched with joy'?)

608 v.3: Here is my robe, my refuge, and my peace –
            Thy blood, thy righteousness, O Lord,
                my God.

642 v.2: That with the world, myself, and thee
            I, ere I sleep, at peace may be.

690 v.3: The sole return thy love requires
            Is that we ask for more.
(But is this true?)

760 v.2: Thy name is life and health and peace
            And everlasting love.

801 v.4: Clothe me with wisdom, patience, love,
            With lowliness and purity.

Single lines:

28 v.5:   Our Maker, Defender, Redeemer, and Friend.
(Note also v.6, with particular attention to the adjectives:
'O *measureless* Might, *ineffable* Love'.)

42 v.2:   To heal, to comfort, and to bless.
(Is there any significance to be found in the order here?)

75 v.3:   Make us humble in believing.

296 v.5: And set up his kingdom of love in the heart
(as elaborated in v.6).

404 v.3: When self-giving is a measure of the greatness of
            the great.

405 v.3: Low lies the best till lifted up to heaven (elaborated in the two following lines).

411 v.1: In Christ we see love's glory consummated (perhaps coupled with the next line).

430 v.1: Each day a judgement day.

519 v.2: Our Prophet, Priest, Redeemer, Lord.
(Is the order here significant or fortuitous?)

529 v.1: The kingdom of an inward heaven.

573 v.1: [lost] In wonder, love and praise
(also 267 v.3).

632 v.2: Redeem thy misspent moments past.
(But is it ever possible to 'redeem' lost time or opportunities? More feasible, perhaps, is the injunction that follows, to 'Live this day as if thy last'; but how many Christians, even, in our hedonistic society will be found ready to take it seriously?)

744 v.3: 'Tis life, and health, and peace.

744 v.4: He breaks the power of *cancelled sin*.

766 v.4: Wisdom, and might, and love are thine.

You will find other examples scattered throughout the rest of this book, but there are many more left for you to discover as you explore the hymn book for yourself.

5

SCRIPTURE

There are obvious links between Scripture and the hymns we sing. Hymn books like the music edition of *Hymns & Psalms* that provide an index of scriptural references are especially helpful in this respect. Metrical paraphrases were among the earliest forms of Protestant hymn-writing, replacing the Prayer Book version of the Psalms in the Scottish Kirk and other Churches in the Reformed tradition, which long held to the principle that there must be scriptural warrant for everything in Christian worship and no place for purely human compositions. Isaac Watts brought a new degree of freedom and greater skill to his Christian adaptation of some of the Psalms. Charles Wesley followed close on his heels and, as has often been noted, his intimate acquaintance with the Bible is reflected in both the subject matter and the language of his hymns. But the difference between these writers and their fellows is only one of degree or intensity. Very few if any hymns have no biblical resonances at all, but in some they are more overt than in others. In these days of diminishing knowledge of the Bible, compounded by the variety of modern versions at our disposal, the 'average' worshipper may well be unaware of much of the biblical language and allusions, and it could be one of our tasks as preachers to identify and expound some of these for our congregations.

Before we wade into deeper water, let us begin by paddling. One feature of the simpler forms of contemporary hymn-writing is the more or less verbatim use of biblical passages. This can be very effective, as in *HP* 137, which consists of little more than the Johannine sayings of Jesus about himself. But v.2 raises the question: how far are we justified in *augmenting* the words of Jesus as recorded in the Gospel? True, this series of 'I am' sayings is so distinctive of the Fourth Gospel, and so markedly different from Jesus' teaching as recorded in the Synoptic Gospels, that we can by no means be sure that they were ever uttered as they stand by Jesus himself. All the same, the addition of 'for the poor' in v.2 is a significant qualification of Jesus' statement, quite unsupported by either John 10:7 or John 14:6. The addition is no doubt understandable enough in the light of the hymn's third world origin where it would have a much greater poignancy and relevance than for affluent Westerners, and it is certainly in line with Jesus' attitude towards the disadvantaged in general, not to mention the positive bias of the Old Testament prophets towards the poor of *their* day. But since most of us who stand up in church to sing these words are scarcely 'poor' by the standards of the world as a whole, are we excluding ourselves from among those for whom Christ is the 'door of the sheep' and the 'way, the truth and the life'?

To determine whether such a comment is mere carping over details, we might compare it with another example in *HP* 216. Charles Wesley's hymn 'And can it be . . .' is so familiar to us that we may not even notice that in the line 'Emptied himself *of all but love*' he has introduced a significant qualification of the divine *kenosis* proclaimed by Paul in Philippians 2:7. If we take this in our stride, should we not do the same with *HP* 137? My own answer would be 'No' – and for two reasons. In the first place, there is a distinction to be made between what are being quoted as, at least purportedly, the words of Christ himself and the words of his apostle. But more importantly, 'of the poor' can be dismissed as an unwarranted narrowing of Christ's words; whereas we may recognise that Wesley's qualifying phrase is in line with the general thrust of Paul's words, not to say the New Testament as a whole. In fact, it amounts to a profound reflection on the nature of the Incarnation, with implications for our understanding of Jesus' ministry which we cannot pursue at this point. Whatever the individual verdict on this, I do not see how any thinking worshippers can avoid noting such details and pondering them for themselves *as part of their worship*; that is, if our hymn-singing is not to resemble the hypnotic repetition of a mantra, which in some Christian quarters it seems to have come uncomfortably close to being.

A more extensive, and more successful, use of a biblical passage is Albert Bayly's paraphrase of Micah 6:6-8 in *HP* 414: a timeless message, as he says:

> Still down the ages ring
> The prophet's stern commands.

The application of the message in vv2-4 to specific sections of society serves to anchor God's demands in the down-to-earth, practical situation of our dealings with others in daily life. It does not matter that some of us are neither merchants, workers nor kings; we can readily apply the principles for ourselves to whatever our own circumstances may be. But, as the closing verse reminds us, we can only meet such demanding standards in our daily living if we are strengthened by grace, a reminder that carries us significantly beyond the original message of the prophet.

The ways in which a passage of Scripture may be used in a hymn differ not only with how familiar it is, but with the genre to which it belongs: poetry or prose, history or epistle, mythology or legend, prophecy or apocalyptic vision? There is a particular risk to be faced by a writer making use of what we now recognise as myth (by which, of course, we do not mean the opposite of truth, but truth expressed in a certain way). Milton could explore the story of the Garden of Eden in a lengthy epic without ever having to face (or persuade his readers to face) the question whether his material was historical or not. So could the unknown author of that delightful medieval carol, 'Adam lay ybounden', though my enjoyment of it each Christmas is slightly shadowed by the thought that some of those listening to the King's College choir may be misled into thinking that, if they are to take Christianity seriously, they are required even in these days to believe in the Genesis account of the origins of the human race. Such a question did not arise until the development of both modern science and biblical criticism in the last two centuries. We are in one respect impoverished by that development, though greatly enriched in others. The question for the modern hymn-writer, and therefore for us as preachers, may be put like this: Was Pratt Green justified in the risk he took (in *HP* 430, 'What Adam's disobedience cost') in using the biblical myths of Adam and Eve and of Noah, since this could be taken to imply that they were historical accounts of past events, rather than powerful statements of timeless truths? The answer – such are the skill and insight he brings to bear on this material – has to be, 'Yes, he was', but the risk was nonetheless a very real one and a congregation may still need guidance to understand what he is (and is *not*) saying. This applies similarly to a hymn such as *HP* 420, even though here it is more obvious that in the rest of the hymn the story of Adam mentioned in the opening verse (and of Cain in v.2) is being used as a symbol or parable of our own spiritual plight. *HP* 427, 'O lift us up, strong Son of God', is another example of the effective (and clearly non-literal) use of the Genesis myth.

In the case of Pratt Green's hymn, the reassuring safeguards against our taking the story as literal history are to be found in some of the phrases (and the ideas behind them) in the two opening verses. The story of Adam's disobedience (not to mention Eve's!) is an assertion of the timeless truth of 'mankind estranged' from God, the source of our existence, so that, in Pratt Green's telling phrase, 'each day [is] a judgement day'. Verse 2 reinforces this verdict on the human race. Given the opportunity of a second chance, we achieve, by our own efforts, only 'another fallen world' – because it is still an 'unrepentant world'. Have you noticed that nowhere in Genesis or elsewhere does the Bible represent Noah as being humbled by his ordeal? (This omission is particularly noticeable in Hebrews 11:7, where it doesn't suit the writer's purpose at all to draw attention to anything except Noah's obedience!) So far is Noah from being awe-struck or penitent in the wake of his narrow escape from the universal catastrophe that, in a sequel we are careful never to read in church, he degenerates into a drunken sot, a kind of biblical Uncle Silas but without the latter's redeeming sense of humour. The phrase 'unrepentant world' steers our attention away from this unedifying spectacle by broadening it to embrace us all as part of the 'fallen world' and then hurrying on in the second half of the hymn to point to Christ as God's solution to our plight. I never heard Pratt Green preach, but I am sure that he showed as much skill in the pulpit as he did in his hymns.

Timothy Dudley-Smith has made something of a speciality of paraphrasing scriptural passages and his hymns set a standard for others. I have always been intrigued by what seems to me the incongruity of a mixed congregation chanting the Magnificat, Mary's beautiful and moving song of response to what can only be called a uniquely unique event. The scenario is not helped by hearing the comfortably well-off solemnly (but surely unthinkingly?) chanting, 'He hath filled the hungry with good things; and the rich he hath sent empty away.' There is a point beyond which even unconscious hypocrisy becomes intolerable. But *HP* 86 miraculously transforms the heart of the Magnificat, gives it a universality lacking in the original and makes it meaningful for 21st-century worshippers. *HP* 279 is another example of his enviable gift, as are *HP* 57, 60 and 507, each based on a Psalm.

There are a number of hymns based on particular incidents in the ministry of Jesus. These, I find, vary considerably in their effectiveness and their usefulness in suggesting ways of treating the gospel stories in a sermon. Many betray their Victorian origin by a degree of sentimentality that has lost much of its appeal. They have dated, like the once popular biblical paintings of Harold Copping. Take, for example, the hymns based on the call of the first disciples, usually treated as a paradigm of our calling to discipleship. In the case of Mrs Alexander's

'Jesus calls us' (*HP* 141), the editors have at least spared us the 'sweet voice' of the original; but even 'clear voice' does not quite exorcise the image of an invitation to a pleasant picnic (or at best the ringing tones of a class teacher on a school outing), rather than a stern challenge to venture into the unknown. A sermon on Christian commitment might well begin by asking, 'Was it at all like this for the Galilean fishermen who left all to follow him?'

Much the same may be said of 'Dear Lord and Father of mankind' by John Greenleaf Whittier (*HP* 673). This has deserved its popularity, since there are helpful thoughts here, not least the reminder of our need for the 'still dews of quietness' in an age of increasingly noisy and frenetic activity. (The general neglect by Christians of the practice of meditation and contemplation goes a long way to explain the attraction of Eastern religions to many in the hyperactive West.) Nevertheless, the hymn as a whole is suffused with Victorian sentimentality and we need to examine more closely such phrases as '*simple* trust' (v.2), and 'the *tender* whisper of thy call' (v.4). Verse 3 is, at best, one-sided in its depiction of what little we are able to gather about Jesus' inner life from the gospels and ignores the evidence of heart-searching and inner turmoil of which we have occasional glimpses. All the same, I would dearly love to hear a sermon on those words in v.3, whose meaning I am as yet far from fully unpacking:

> The silence of eternity
> Interpreted by love.

If I were preaching on those lines myself, I would certainly want to define and qualify what they seem to be saying, asking 'Why "silence"?', and 'Is it the silence or eternity itself that is being "interpreted"?' As soon as we begin to look for meaning in this hymn, the language becomes unexpectedly vague, like a badly focused photograph, and prompts one question after another. What did Whittier mean by our being 'reclothed' in our rightful mind? (Something like 'Restore us to . . .' would surely be nearer the mark.) Can Christ's call really be drowned by 'our words and works', and if so, in what circumstances? (That itself would be worth pursuing in the pulpit.) I also have serious disquiet about the desire for 'all our strivings' to cease, so that 'our ordered lives' may 'confess the beauty of thy peace' (v.5). If this is the proper goal of Christian devotion, then I find myself sharing the early Methodist misgivings about 'stillness' and am inclined to say, 'In that case, count me out.' That Whittier's language is quite a long way from the language and thought of the Bible itself may be judged by the closing allusion to Elijah on Mount Horeb. I find no suggestion in 1 Kings 19 that his sense(s) became 'dumb' or that his flesh 'retired' (whatever those words may be taken to mean). And the voice of God (in his case, one of rebuke and challenge, and by no means 'of calm') spoke to him not *through* the earthquake, wind and fire, but in the hush that *followed* them. The verse seems for the most part to be going against the grain of the biblical story, not extrapolating from it. We will see what Charles Wesley makes of it later.

The strength of William Walsham How's 'Behold a little child' (*HP* 143), and even more of George W Briggs' 'Son of the Lord most high' (*HP* 152), lies in the way they relate the death of Jesus to the years that preceded it. (A similar link is made in *HP* 177 and in *HP* 164 v.4.) All too often we have interpreted Calvary in isolation from the life to which it was a climax, and so, as I will suggest elsewhere, have been in danger of misinterpreting it in our various 'doctrines of the atonement'. *HP* 152 at least offers us an opportunity to see his death in the context of his life and should discourage us from seeing it as no more than a reckless and futile gesture of defiance. Verse 2 in particular also helps us to recognise the common humanity we share with him and goes a little way towards compensating for the loss of Henry Van Dyke's hymn, 'They who tread the path of labour' (*MHB* 601), with its echo of one of the few surviving apocryphal sayings of Jesus: 'Raise the stone and thou shalt find Me; cleave the wood and I am there.'[1]

The hymns which deal with Jesus' healing ministry tend to interpret it metaphorically, with the physical illnesses of those he cured becoming symbols of our spiritual ailments and needs. *HP* 148, 'Jesus, thy far-extended fame', is an example of this: Jesus 'the good, the kind physician' who was kept so busy during his earthly ministry restoring the body's health, does not disregard 'the sin-sick soul' which he loves even more. (*HP* 142 and 150 are other examples.) The hymn ends by extending the metaphor:

> In pardon, Lord, my cure begin,
> And perfect it in holiness.

Charles Wesley is not prepared, any more than his brother, for us to regain our spiritual health only to sit back and take no steps towards improving it further. This could certainly be elaborated into a challenge to every Christian to 'press on towards the goal . . . of our high calling in Christ Jesus' (Philippians 3:14). (For an extended exposition of this theme, see *HP* 747, which begins by addressing the 'Saviour from sin' by his 'healing name' of Jesus.)

Verse 4 of *HP* 150 makes a passing reference to the healing of the man at the Pool of Bethesda (John 5:1-9). Perhaps the most interesting detail in this story is the question Jesus asks in v.6: 'Do you want to be healed?' Without directly alluding to this detail in the story, Wesley suggests the explanation of why Jesus should have asked what seems so unnecessary and even insensitive a question. The hymn as a whole is an acknowledgement of our need of Christ. So long as we are convinced that we are among those who 'have no need of a physician' (Mark 2:17), we deny ourselves access to his healing (or saving) power. The first step the Prodigal had to take in returning to his father's house was to recognise the mess he had made of his life and to accept the responsibility for it. Only by similarly recognising and acknowledging our need of Christ can we enable him to save us from what the hymn calls 'the most inveterate plague' of all. Confession, in whatever form it may take, remains as essential a part of our worship as ever.

'When Jesus the healer passed through Galilee' (*HP* 151) appears to be built on the same parallel between physical and spiritual sickness, though not so explicitly that one can be sure. I am not entirely confident that worshippers would be clear about what they were actually pleading for in the reiterated 'Heal us today!' And despite the allusion to a whole series of gospel stories, what is notable is that, in contrast with the hymns mentioned above, the author *does nothing with them* beyond piling them up as examples, whether literally of physical healings or metaphorically of salvation from sin. So the hymn amounts to little more than a useful reminder of some of the gospel stories at a time of widespread ignorance of the Bible. You will find a great deal more food for thought in Pratt Green's 'O Christ, the Healer, we have come' (*HP* 395), where the direct reference to physical illness is not shunned, but is seen in the wider context of our need for 'wholeness' (v.2). We are not souls temporarily inhabiting bodies, but a single entity uniting both physical and psychological in the potential 'wholeness' of which this hymn speaks.

As a postscript to this, note how the emphasis in a hymn like *HP* 440, 'Omnipotent Redeemer, our ransomed souls adore thee' is on our being not 'miserable' but *pardoned* sinners, with good reason for exulting in Christ's power to save. The gospel we proclaim offers not only a diagnosis, but also a remedy for the deepest of human needs. We are not doomed, any more than Bunyan's pilgrim, to carry the burden of sin through the whole of life's journey, even though we need to seek forgiveness again and again.

Although the concept of 'miracle' is more problematical in a scientific age than it was in the past, our understanding of psychosomatic illness makes it easier for us to understand and accept the healing miracles of Jesus; provided, of course, we do not assume that once we are able to understand the causes of an event it thereby ceases to be 'miraculous'. Our understanding of the meaning of both 'miracle' and 'natural law' is crucial here, not least for our presentation of the claims of Christianity to the uncommitted. In this respect, the so-called 'nature miracles' (walking on water, stilling a storm, etc.) present more serious problems to our scientifically conditioned minds. One solution has been to find natural, rather than supernatural, explanations of what originally happened. But for some that involves even larger problems about the truth and reliability of the Bible. In view of this, it is perhaps hardly surprising that hymn-writers have made much less use of these 'nature miracles'; or that when they do use them, they are inclined to side-step the problem by treating the event allegorically. *HP* 144, 'Fierce raged the tempest o'er the deep', does this in the case of Jesus stilling the storm (Mark 4:36-41 etc.), treating it purely as an allegory of the storms that threaten our daily lives. In order to sing the hymn, we do not need to make up our minds about whether the sudden cessation of the storm on the Sea of Galilee was a miracle or a natural coincidence. The allegory works in either case. But 'Eternal Father, strong to save' (*HP* 379) is quite a different matter, since it makes explicit statements about God's control over the oceans and their storms and raises the question of how far we can afford to distance ourselves from the 'real' world as presented to us by our senses and interpreted by our reason. There are times when the words we sing come close to 'whistling in the dark'. What else, for example, is the line in H F Lyte's popular 'Praise, my soul, the King of heaven' (*HP* 13), which states that he 'rescues us from all our foes'? But to recognise this is no more than to acknowledge that we are human and sometimes need the equivalent of Linus's blanket.

By their very nature, parables lend themselves more readily to the needs of the hymn-writer, though the number of examples of their use is quite few in *Hymns & Psalms*. *HP* 460, 'Come, sinners, to the gospel feast' is a quite straightforward application of the parable of the 'great supper' in Luke 14:16-24; it adds relatively little to the parable itself, beyond making explicit what is merely implied there. If we are thinking about the words as we sing them, we might momentarily query the verb 'compel' in v.4, but only to recall that the word is taken straight from Luke, where the servants are instructed to 'compel' or 'constrain' those they find in the highways and hedges to come to the banquet. It is worth noting that the subject of 'compel' is not any kind of power or authority, but Christ's *love*, just as later in the same verse it is *'love's power'* that is described as 'resistless', as if to say that for the Christian no other restraint is either acceptable or effective. One further comment on this hymn may be worth making. In John Wesley's 1780 Hymn Book it is placed second in the collection, immediately following 'O for a thousand tongues' (*HP* 744), and both hymns belong to the opening section entitled 'Exhorting and beseeching [unbelievers or 'backsliders'] to return to God'. So in Wesley's view, both hymns were evangelical in intent and assumed the presence of the unconverted among the congregation, in contrast to the inward-looking mind-set of most of today's congregations. 'O for a thousand tongues' has now been demoted from its traditional place as the first hymn in the book and, even more significantly, is to be found in a section entitled 'Growth in grace and holiness'. Even the restoration of v.6, with its powerful evocation of Isaiah 35:5-6,

> Hear him, ye deaf; his praise, ye dumb,
> Your loosened tongues employ;
> Ye blind, behold your Saviour come;
> And leap, ye lame, for joy!

in which the evangelical tenor is bold and clear, does not disguise the way in which what was originally designed ' for export has been commandeered by the domestic market.

Four successive hymns (*HP* 155-158) are based on the story of the Transfiguration, that enigmatic turning-point in Christ's ministry. The first three are new, Samuel Greg's 'Stay, Master, stay upon this heavenly hill' (*HP* 158) being the only survivor from the 1933 *Methodist Hymn Book*. It would be a useful exercise to examine this group of hymns in order to consider which most authentically or effectively interprets the Transfiguration in a way that makes it meaningful for us today. Certainly v.2 of *HP* 158 catches something of the bewilderment of those who were there. But *HP* 157, 'Once on a mountain top', suggests to me more lines of thought worth exploring, reminding us in particular that in spite of the materialism of our scientific and technological age there are still 'things which lie beyond our sight'. These are no less real for our being blinded by the reductionist assumptions of our day. I am not, on the other hand, at all happy with 'They watched the wheels of nature stop' (v.1), which suggests an out-dated contrast between 'natural' and 'supernatural', rather than an interpenetration of different levels of reality. We have surely got beyond the concept of the supernatural kicking in at the point where the natural lapses. Understandably, there is nothing in these hymns to help us make up our minds about the nature of the apparitions which the disciples identified as Moses and Elijah; but that is an aspect of the story we can scarcely ignore if we choose to preach on this incident. In the end, our choice between these four hymns must surely depend on how far each succeeds in expressing the uniqueness of the disciples' mountain-top experience, in terms not of its being unparalleled, but of its depth of insight into a reality beyond our physical senses.

Does any of this matter to the average member of our congregations (if such a person exists)? I am sure it does, if we want them, through our preaching as well as through their reading of the Bible, to sharpen their understanding of Christian truth and their own calling. Jesus himself rebuked his disciples on occasions for their slowness to understand his words and what was happening before their eyes. Should we set any lower standard?

Finally, I am compelled yet again to take examples from Charles Wesley. As has often been pointed out, his hymns are saturated in biblical language. Take *HP* 745, 'O thou who camest from above', in which no fewer than 25 biblical references, from both Old and New Testaments, have been noted. This is by no means exceptional.

However, more to our present point is the fact that some of Wesley's greatest hymns take the form of extended meditations on biblical stories. It is interesting, and perhaps significant, that these are usually from the Old Testament, but treated allegorically as a means of exploring the Christian experience of God. Generally regarded as his greatest hymn, highly praised by no other than Isaac Watts and, more surprisingly, earning a place in the *Oxford Book of Christian Verse*, is 'Wrestling Jacob' (*HP* 434). The story of the exiled Jacob's encounter with a mysterious stranger as he prepares to meet the brother he cheated many years earlier (Genesis 32:22-32) becomes an allegory of the Christian's wrestling in prayer with God. More specifically, indeed, it depicts our struggle to plumb the depths of a mystery – that of a God 'whose nature and name is love'. This carries us far beyond any glib parrot-like repetition of 1 John 4:8, 'God is love' and recognises that in all our lives there are times of sorrow and bewilderment when it is hard indeed to discern the love of God at work, and to believe that he himself *is* love. The editors of *Hymns & Psalms* have bravely given us the full 12 verses of this tremendous hymn and left us to make of it what we can. Certainly it cries out to be expounded and in attempting this we may make it easier for a congregation if we divide it into shorter and more manageable parts. This is not easily done, but a progression *can* be discerned in the hymn. Verses 1-5 express the bafflement, frustration, and even despair, that may sometimes overwhelm us in the face of life and our own inadequacy (and, at a deeper level, our sinfulness). At that stage we may even have no name for what, or who, it is we are dealing with. Verse 6 is the pivotal verse, where for the first time is expressed the possibility that, against all appearances, we may after all be confronted by one whose name is Love. And v.7 opens with a triumphant cry at the discovery that this is indeed so. From this point on the hymn becomes a rhapsody on the fact that his 'nature and his name is Love'. It is the death of Christ on the cross (not the beauty of nature, nor any human virtue) that reveals this divine love to us (v.7). This discovery that love is at the heart of the universe gives us confidence in prayer (v.8), because we can pray in and through the name of the one whom we now know as 'the sinner's friend' (v.9). This new relationship with him heralds the dawn of a new life (v.10), in which we depend no longer on our own strength, but on his grace (v.11) and so are no longer defeated, but triumph in and through his love (v.12).

I do not know that it has ever been noticed that the climax of this hymn is in effect a versification of words Charles' brother wrote at the end of his account of his Aldersgate Street experience:

> After my return home, I was much buffeted with temptations; but cried out, and they fled away. They returned again and again. I as often lifted up my eyes, and He 'sent me help from His holy place'. And herein I found the difference between this and my former state chiefly consisted. I was striving, yea fighting with all my might under the law, as well as under grace. But then I was sometimes, if not often, conquered; now I was always conqueror.

Or, as Paul put it in Romans 8:37, 'We are more than conquerors through him that loved us.'

To tackle such a theme, and to do so through a hymn such as 'Wrestling Jacob' is no trivial undertaking. But there are times, surely, when for our own sake as well as for our congregation's, we should be prepared for our reach to exceed our grasp, or, as Browning's Andrea del Sarto asked, 'What's a heaven for?'

Second only to 'Wrestling Jacob' in this respect is Wesley's meditation in *HP* 540 on Elijah's encounter with God on Mount Horeb (1 Kings 19). The prophet has taken refuge on the sacred mountain during a failure of nerve following his triumph over the prophets of Baal. These historical circumstances do not concern Wesley, any more than the sequel in which Elijah is sent by God to instigate what becomes a bloody and ruthless revolt led by Jehu against the royal house of Ahab. He concentrates on the rather more edifying details of how the prophet regained his nerve by hearing God speaking to him in the solitude and silence of the mountain top. Once again it is not long before the Old Testament story brings Wesley to the foot of the cross, which represents 'wisdom in a mystery of bleeding love' (v.3). This brings him, in turn, face to face with the reality of his own 'inbred sin' (a more acceptable and less readily misunderstood term, surely, than 'original sin' for our human plight), including 'unbelief' and 'pride' and those aspirations, however innocent or even praiseworthy in the eyes of the world, that will not be subject to Christ's rule (v.4). And so to a climax in v.5, which is perhaps the most searching self-surrender to the divine will ever penned. The age of subservience has been so completely swept away that we are inclined to treat even God as an equal, rather than one to whom we must submit life, being and will. Wesley's hymn may help us to recover the dimension of our spiritual life we have largely lost in these egalitarian days.

Once we start looking for them, there are many words and phrases in the hymns we sing which derive from the Bible and so provide opportunities for us to explore and expound the Scriptures, sometimes from a fresh angle. But a scriptural basis is no guarantee in itself of a successful hymn. Despite its allusion to the appearances of the risen Jesus at Emmaus and in the upper room in Jerusalem, *HP* 199, 'Jesus, Lord, Redeemer', seems limp and dispirited in comparison with the joyful exhilaration of the other Easter hymns. Maybe it was included for the sake of those who are so 'desolate and weary', overburdened or defeated by life, that they are unable to join in the celebration. If so, it seems to me a poor substitute for *MHB* 320, 'Art thou weary, art thou languid?', which is one of the hymns omitted from *Hymns & Psalms*.

NOTE

1   Found among the sayings of Jesus in the collection of papyri
    discovered at Oxyrhynchus in Egypt.

6

CHRISTMASTIDE

A dvent

Clearly, there is only one place to begin a review of the Christian Year. The various themes of Advent, the season of expectation and preparation, are rehearsed in *HP* 88, 'The holly and the ivy', and now often used in association with the lighting of the Advent candles. The traditional carol from which this new version takes its opening line may be equally doggerel from a literary point of view, but it at least has resonances, deriving from childhood memories, which the new version lacks. Other Advent hymns have a longer pedigree and richer biblical associations, and so offer food for thought at this season. 'The race that long in darkness pined' (*HP* 89) is one of the more successful of the Scottish paraphrases and, like Philip Doddridge's freer paraphrasing in *HP* 82, 'Hark the glad sound!', highlights the important role of prophecy in Christian tradition. In v.4 of Doddridge's hymn our worship echoes, however faintly, the eternal worship of heaven. Set to a traditional tune that is eminently singable, Pratt Green's 'Long ago, prophets knew' (*HP* 83) explores the central Advent theme from a variety of points of view.

Once again, Charles Wesley turns up trumps, if such an idiom is permitted in Methodist circles! In 'Come, thou long-expected Jesus' (*HP* 81) he begins with the Messianic hope of Israel, fulfilled, but not at all in the way the Israelite nation expected, since the Messiah when he came was a liberator not from political or military subjugation, but from 'our fears and sins'. It is interesting to note how in v.2 the focus expands and contracts, starting with the Israelite nation, widening to embrace 'all the earth' and 'every nation' on it, and finally focusing down sharply on the individual. Which is the more wonderful, that the grace of God in Christ should be all-embracing, or that it should stoop to become the 'joy of every longing heart'? Verses 3 and 4 continue this alternation between the wide-angled and the zoom lens. Christ reigns not just throughout the universe, but 'in all our hearts' and 'alone' – without a rival, so long as we open them to his 'eternal Spirit'.

But the soaring pinnacle among the Advent hymns is also the oldest. 'O come, O come, Immanuel' (*HP* 85) in its Latin original can be traced back over a thousand years and its rich symbolism is firmly rooted in the Old Testament itself. Embedded in the hymn is a wealth of meaning far greater than could possibly be unpacked in a single sermon. Judicious selection or a series of three or four Advent meditations are the only ways we might begin to do justice to it.

As we have it in John Mason Neale's translation, what is now the opening verse originally came at the end of the Latin antiphons known as the 'great O's', but its firm grounding in biblical imagery and the significance for Christians of the Hebrew name Immanuel more than justifies its place at the beginning of the hymn, where it vividly sets the mood of eager hope. We must remember that one image of the Church used by the early Christians was that of the 'new Israel'. This among other things implied that she inherited God's promises to Israel of old and could confidently look for the fulfilment of ancient prophecies.

In the original version, Christ is described as 'the hope of the Gentiles and their Saviour'. Until he arrives, we are like persons exiled from their true home. The name Immanuel, 'God is with us', was part of the sign given by the prophet Isaiah to King Ahaz at the height of a national emergency (Isaiah 7:14). Jerusalem was in imminent danger of falling to its Assyrian besiegers. The sign offered by the prophet involved no miraculous birth (the Hebrew word means merely a young woman, not a virgin as the Greek of the Septuagint implies), but only the miracle of faith, expressed by the mother-to-be in the name she would give to her child. '*Only* the miracle of faith'? Her faith, said Isaiah, would be speedily vindicated, putting to shame the king's lack of confidence in 'the arm of the Lord'. Nothing minimalist there.

It is interesting to see how Matthew's Gospel reinterprets the original sign, influenced on the one hand by the highly significant name 'Immanuel' and on the other by the Septuagint's reference to a virgin mother. We may see it, not so much as 'proof' through a prophecy fulfilled (as it appeared to earlier generations) but rather as new and deeper insight into ancient words and actions. King Ahaz lived in a time of crisis, when it was not easy to put your trust in God. There have been many such times of crisis since, down to our own lifetime. So the prophet's message of hope is a message for us too.

'O Adonai, Ruler of the house of Israel, who didst appear unto Moses in the burning bush and gavest him the law on Sinai, come to redeem us . . .' These are the words, translated from the Latin original, that lie behind the second verse of Neale's hymn. In highlighting the numinous details ('cloud and majesty and awe') of the scene at Sinai, Neale reminds us of an aspect of worship we are sometimes in danger of forgetting in these days of casual relationships. But in doing this he has sacrificed another aspect of the original which is of some significance. The God of the Old Testament and the New (whatever differences of insight and understanding may need to be taken into account) are one God, both Lawgiver and Redeemer. One of the earliest Christian heresies, Marcionism, taught that with the coming of Jesus as the Messiah the Old Testament was no longer valid and should be discarded. True, there are things in the Old Testament which we must firmly repudiate in the light of God's revelation of himself in Christ, and we should be more honest with our congregations about that, when the need arises. But as preachers we also need to be clear that, far from being superseded, the 'old' and the 'new' revelations are complementary and interdependent. And one of the valuable emphases of the Old Testament is on the awe-ful majesty of God. If we don't begin there, we shall, at the very least, miss the sense of wonder that such a being should 'call himself my friend' and, as already noted, may slip into the over-casual style that characterises some contemporary so-called worship.

Neale's treatment of the scene at Sinai, however brief, also reminds us, at least by implication, that in one important respect Moses was characteristic of many other biblical figures. If mysticism is a search for God's presence for its own sake, then there is surprisingly little of it in the Bible. For one thing, it is always *God* who initiates. Furthermore, not only Moses, but Noah, Abram, Gideon, Samuel, Amos, Isaiah, Jeremiah, Paul on the Damascus road, Peter at Joppa . . . these and others all found that when God revealed himself to them he did so *with a purpose*. Usually it was to challenge and make demands on them. So it was with Moses. The voice that spoke to him from the midst of the burning bush was the voice of his conscience, through which God sent him back to Egypt to identify himself with his oppressed brethren. As a result, Judaism became a religion of moral obedience, however far short the people of Israel may have fallen again and again. The Law was seen as God's gift for which his people gave thanks. To a Jew, the Torah is both Law *and* revelation, an expression of God's will and also of his nature.

Centuries later the same was true of Jesus. In him people found the true nature of God revealed to them – but only if they were prepared to respond to the challenge he embodied. According to John, this was spelled out by Jesus himself in the upper room, when he told his disciples, 'He who has my commandments and keeps them, he it is who loves me . . . and I will love him and manifest myself to him' (John 14:21). So what God says to us, whether during Advent or any other season in the

Christian year, may depend on how far we have responded to the vision already vouchsafed us.

In v.3 the image of the rod (or 'shoot') of Jesse is drawn from Isaiah 11:1-10 and refers to a descendant of the royal house of David. Stripped of its later Christian overtones, the passage still offers a remarkable and moving vision. It depicts a future age in which not only human beings but all God's creatures would be freed from the afflictions and conflicts that mar their present existence; and this would happen through a common allegiance to the expected Messianic king. Verse 10 is thought to belong to a later period than the rest, perhaps to the years following the Exile in Babylon. It marks a significant broadening and deepening of the earlier vision, in that God's purposes are now seen as embracing not just 'the people of God', but those of all nations.

The early Christians in their turn claimed that, as befitted the Messiah, Jesus was of the 'blood royal'. In him, as the prophet put it, a fresh shoot had sprung out of the seemingly dead 'stump' which was all that was left of the royal house of David. To him people of all nations would rally as to a battle standard, a prophecy fulfilled in the spread of Christianity throughout the world. So a vision vouchsafed to the old nation of Israel was realised in and through the 'new Israel' of the Church as it broke the narrow confines of nationality.

However, a sense of vocation has its own built-in temptation. The new Israel, like the old, had to learn that God had not singled her out as the object of special favour, but rather for witness and service ('We have no mission but to serve . . .'), to be the means by which *all* people might be drawn to him. It is fatally easy for our vision to become narrow and parochial, or to imagine that God's purposes are circumscribed by our own schemes and plans. If he has singled us out, it is not for special favour, but as before for witness and service.

The 'Key of David' in v.4 takes us back to passages in both Old and New Testaments. Isaiah 22:15-25 is, at first sight, a pretty uninspiring and unedifying account of palace intrigue in Jerusalem. We read of how Eliakim ousted his rival as doorkeeper of the royal audience chamber (presumably quite a lucrative post). As a badge of his new office he was given the 'key of David'. Henceforth he, not the deposed Shebna, was the one who had to be 'squared' by anyone seeking admittance to the king's presence.

This unpromising material had to wait centuries before it was transformed by a kind of alchemy into a shining symbol in the Book of Revelation. In Revelation 3:7 Jesus is declared to be the one who has used the 'key of David' to provide us with an ever-open door which gives access to the 'new Jerusalem' of God's own presence. So no one and nothing can debar us from the God who makes himself known to us in Jesus Christ (who, in the hymn, becomes not just the key-holder, but the Key itself). We may well detect echoes of Paul's declaration that nothing in all creation 'will be able to separate us from the love of God in Christ Jesus our Lord' (Romans 8:38-39). The key which in the hands of Eliakim could be used either to admit or to debar has become a symbol of the privilege of free access to our heavenly King.

But the same symbol of a key also suggests an entirely different line of thought: that of release from imprisonment. It was a key labelled 'Promise' that freed Christian and Hopeful from the castle of Giant Despair – which might equally have stood for enslavement to sin in Bunyan's allegory. So the picture conjured up is of a prisoner stumbling on the threshold of his newly gained freedom, blinded by the daylight to which his eyes have become unaccustomed, yet overjoyed to discover that life still holds promise of joy and fulfilment. If we follow this line of thought, we again have an Old Testament symbol (Isaiah 42:6-7) picked up and refurbished in the New (Acts 12:6-9; also 5:19, 26:18 etc.) and given vigorous new lease of life by Charles Wesley ('Long my imprisoned spirit lay, Fast bound in sin and nature's night . . . My chains fell off, my heart was free . . .', *HP* 216). If the gospel still has any relevance in a technological age, it is surely here: in proclaiming that without hope, people are prisoners of their own doubts and fears, shut away from the sunlight and languishing in a purposeless existence; but there *is* an alternative.

Such, certainly, is the upbeat mood of the final verse of this hymn, based on the image of the dawning of a new day. If dawn were an event which occurred only once in every century, millions would sit up all night to see it and anyone who missed it by oversleeping would be written off as impossibly 'dull of soul'. Even as a daily affair, the dawn has the power, as Wordsworth discovered on Westminster Bridge, to clothe the everyday world in beauty. Yet how often do we take pains to watch the sunrise? It is an old story: if gold were as plentiful as sand, how many would reach out a hand to take it?

In this respect, we moderns have something important to learn from our less sophisticated ancestors. Primitive people, though they had not learned to harness it as solar power, were well aware of their dependence on the light and heat of the sun. It became one of their earliest objects of worship, as the source of life itself. Yet, except in the most temperate climates, the sun can be an enemy as well as a friend – relentlessly scorching and destroying life, as desert dwellers know only too well. That it is one and the same sun which both gives and destroys life is a thought that lies behind Malachi 4:1-3, which in turn provides some of the imagery here in v.5.

So sunrise is an event to be dreaded by those who have no shelter from its burning rays; but it is also a symbol of hope. If for some the dawn means renewed bitterness, the resumption of life's struggle and burdens, the facing of problems from which sleep has provided a brief respite, for others it brings a new beginning, fresh opportunities and joys. For them, 'Morning has broken, like the *first* morning' (*HP* 635). Or, as the older hymn says, 'New mercies each returning day hover around us while we pray' (*HP* 636). The Christian is not spared that 'dark night of the soul' of which the mystics speak. There will be times when God seems remote or unreal: did not

Christ himself have to experience Gethsemane? But we can always look forward with hope to the coming dawn, when the 'sun of righteousness' will arise 'with healing in his wings'. Once again, fulfilment of a long-cherished dream finds fulfilment in the New Testament, when Zechariah hails the Christ child as the one through whom 'the day shall dawn upon us from on high to give light to those who sit in darkness and in the shadow of death' (Luke 1:78-79).

Which brings us to the Christmas season itself.

Christmas

It is hard to decide what we should do about Christmas, as a Christian festival that is. It is as though we have come to value the fancy wrappings so highly that we have mislaid the gift they enclosed. Maybe there is very little we *can* do, apart from abandoning it as a lost cause. At least it could then be enjoyed for its own sake as a secular festival of sentimentality and self-indulgence, plus a certain amount of targeted good will. In some parts of Europe, such as the Netherlands, they seem to handle it better by concentrating much of the razzle-dazzle on 6th December, the feast day of St Nicholas, but it seems unlikely that the great British public would be fobbed off with such a solution, even if commercial interests were not also at stake.

It does disturb me when youngsters at the door can only offer me a rendering of 'Rudolph, the red-nosed reindeer' and are perplexed when I protest that is not, in fact, a Christmas carol. They are, no doubt, representatives of the consumerism of a secular age. But the fact that their motivation is a purely mercenary one is of relatively little consequence: in that respect they are merely following, however unawares, the example of generations of Christmas mummers. The heart of the problem, however, lies much deeper than that. My more serious concern kicks in when I consider what alternative to this the Church has on offer. Judging by our public services at this Christmas season, our response amounts to little more than sentimentality and unquestioned folklore. By the time we have accommodated gift services and other forms of family worship (all legitimate in themselves) and organised the annual carol service, with even perhaps a nativity play thrown in for good measure, the festival of Christ's nativity has come and gone; and once again we seem to have found no room at the inn for any serious consideration of its real meaning. Nor, with shepherds and wise men jockeying for position around the Bethlehem manger, is there much left for us to make use of at Epiphany, as we shall see.

Part of the trouble is surely that we do not recognise and acknowledge clearly enough the very clear distinction, historically speaking, between the nativity stories in Matthew and Luke and the records of Jesus' ministry that occupy the rest of the Synoptic Gospels. We are so concerned not to sow seeds of doubt in what we tend to think of as the 'simple minds' of our congregations that I strongly suspect we achieve quite the opposite of what we intend. By being left, unquestioned and uninterpreted, to 'speak for itself', the Christmas story is neatly pigeon-holed for those outside the Church, and even for many of the faithful, as just another a fairy tale.

This was brought home to me some years ago when the Chichester Festival Theatre put on as its Christmas show a musical retelling of the Nativity story, using much the same format as a pantomime. Great fun, and in places very moving, and unquestionably successful in enlisting the wholehearted participation of the younger element in the audience. No question of its being in bad taste or even blasphemous in its novel presentation of the traditional material. But one misgiving lingered on after the performance and has not yet quite gone away. For how many of the audience, both old and young, would it have reinforced a half-conscious assumption that the story was on a par with those fairy tales which form the basis of our Christmas pantomimes? How many could, or would, have made the leap of faith that anchors the birth of Christ firmly in the real world in which our daily lives are lived?

If we confine our choice of Christmas hymns to those traditional carols which do little more than retell the story with popular embellishments, much loved and rightly cherished as they are, and never challenge our congregations to launch out into deeper metaphysical and spiritual waters, are we not failing them at a crucial point in their growth as Christians and risking their repudiation of a faith they may come to see as childish?

Better, surely, to help people come to terms with the idea that we are dealing here, not with sober historical fact, but with devout legends which are to be treasured because they bear witness in their own way to the uniqueness of Jesus and his relationship to God, as seen through the eyes of the earliest generations of Christians. By all means let us make sure that the first Nowell rings afresh in our jaded modern ears each Christmastide, and that we follow both 'certain poor shepherds' and 'wise men from country far' to gaze in wonder and adoration at 'the little Lord Jesus asleep on the hay'. But dare we leave it there?

When did you last hear (or preach) a sermon on the meaning of the Incarnation, the stupendous – or preposterous according to your standpoint – claim that the divine Being, the ultimate Reality and Source of all existence in and beyond our universe, became a human being by means of a natural human birth on this inconspicuous planet, and yet remained God? It's hardly surprising if, to a majority of our contemporaries in our hard-bitten, prosaic Western world, this is either a charming but irrelevant folk tale or simple nonsense. The choice is a stark one: either it is no more than that, or else it is, as John Betjeman says, the 'most tremendous tale of all'. And if it *is* that, then none of the tinselly trappings with which we have festooned the season

> Can with this single Truth compare –
> That God was Man in Palestine,

A truth, some may want to add, compared with which, Betjeman's belief in the 'real presence' of Christ in the

51

sacramental elements may seem secondary, if not debatable.

So where does all this leave us as preachers of the gospel? Is there indeed 'good news' to be proclaimed to the kind of world we find ourselves in at the beginning of a new millennium? Or are we exactly where we found ourselves (those of us whose memory takes us that far back) as we sang amid the blackout and blitzes of wartime winters half a century ago:

> Yet with the woes of sin and strife
> The world has suffered long;
> Beneath the angel strain have rolled
> Two thousand years of wrong. (*HP* 108)?

That at least had a note of realism in it even at the height of a World War, and it still has. It is hard not to conclude that in those 'two thousand years of wrong', Christianity, for all its influence for good in a variety of ways, has been shown to be ineffectual and/or irrelevant when it comes to the big issues. Has God, then, failed? Or are we being reminded that by his own choice he is limited by our response of obedience and discipleship? It is easy for us to look to God to do what we could and should be doing for ourselves; to ask him, indeed, to transform our world not through us, but in spite of our wilfulness and greed – in a word, our sin. Any honest appraisal of our experience of life surely makes it clear that he does not choose to do so. It is no part of his 'universal plan' to play the part of an interventionist God.

HP 108 at least has the virtue of recognising the gulf that yawns between the ideal and the real worlds, so long as 'man at war with man hears not the love-song' of the Bethlehem angels. The predominant note has to be, and must remain, one, not of facile optimism about the present, but of courageous hope for the future. Whether 'the days are *hastening* on' may still be disputed in the face of the evidence. But in the changes they have made to v.4, the editors have at least offered us a more realistic and biblical prospect than that of the return of a mythical 'age of gold' to which the hymn originally referred. The Christmas season may offer an opportunity, not only to look back nostalgically, but to ask more searchingly, 'What of the future?'

One verse in the original hymn (see *MHB* 130 v.4) has been dropped altogether in the present version, perhaps because it was undoubtedly a 'curate's egg' which defied all attempts to rescue it from the kind of glib prevailing optimism that was shattered by World War I. It is a pity that the verse that has been sacrificed includes reference to those (all too numerous in our world) for whom life is a crushing burden beneath which they stumble and fall. These at least should never be far from our minds at Christmas, whatever we may make of the theological conundrums. I for one am grateful to Arnold Kellett who, in his Christmas poems, has again and again challenged us to compassion and generosity in the name of the God who gave himself to us in the supreme act of self-giving of all time.

This, then, is the situation in which we are called to proclaim a Christmas message that is meaningful and relevant, not just to the committed Christians in our congregations, but to anyone else who may inadvertently come within hearing of our preaching at this season. If we can brush aside the tinsel long enough to make ourselves heard above the angelic host, can the Christmas hymns on offer help us to find anything of substance to say about the 'incarnate deity'?

That phrase itself reminds us that we can hardly do better than begin with Charles Wesley, if only we can somehow squeeze him in between all those wall-to-wall carols. And if we do, we shall be inescapably reminded that at the heart of our Christmas celebration, however we interpret the nativity stories, must be an overwhelming sense of wonder, best expressed in the form of paradox. In 'Glory be to God on high' (*HP* 101) one paradox follows hard on the heels of another. Similarly, 'Let earth and heaven combine' (*HP* 109) is redolent with a sense of the incomprehensibility of the very idea of 'our God' being 'contracted to a span' (v.1). This is a self-emptying of immeasurable proportions (v.2) and the love that lies behind it is 'unsearchable'; the grace far above even angels' comprehension (v.3). By bringing together the widest conceivable extremes, his becoming human makes possible what would otherwise be equally inconceivable, that we should become like him (v.4), 'made perfect first in love, and sanctified by grace':

> His love shall then be fully showed,
> And man shall then be lost in God.

The sweeping vision of this concluding couplet makes most of our aspirations and expectations seem prosaic and puny indeed. The closing line brings us face to face with one of the most breathtaking prospects of all. This is one of several occasions when Charles Wesley toys with the concept of 'deification', which he has already put even more explicitly in v.4:

> He deigns in flesh to appear,
>   Widest extremes to join;
> To bring our vileness near,
>   And *make us all divine.*

Here, in its starkest terms, is the idea that God became human in order that we might become divine. If the gulf can be bridged from one side, why not from the other; or rather, is it inconceivable that the traffic on the bridge might be more than one-way? This concept of deification is found in the New Testament only in 2 Peter 1:4, but it was taken up by some of the early Fathers, notably Clement of Alexandria. It has played little part in Western theology, which has been more aware of the risk of misinterpreting and misapplying so daring an idea. On the other hand, it survived in Eastern Orthodox theology and has been taken up in some parts of the Western Church in more recent times. It crops up in one or two other places in Charles Wesley's hymns (though not, I think, in his brother's sermons). We may well ask, has it any place in Methodist preaching, or that of Protestantism generally? Well, set the concept against the depths of depravity into which the human race has descended throughout its history, and not least during the 20th-century and at the very outset of our new millennium, and you have a breathtaking vista against which the traditional images of Christmas may look trivial indeed. I can only compare it with gazing into the Grand Canyon, something that can scarcely be conveyed to anyone who has not experienced it at first hand.

So I come back to the thought that, whatever demythologising may be needed to get to the heart of the Christmas message, in the end what matters and should remain long after the decorations have been taken down is the sense of wonder, nowhere better expressed than in another of Wesley's paradoxes, that

> Being's source begins to be
> And God himself is born! (*HP* 101 v.2)

Time to get our feet back on terra firma and to ask whether there isn't something useful, if more prosaic, to be gained from the lower ranges of the Christmas hymnody, as indeed there is. There is much of value in John Byrom's stately but moving 'Christians, awake' (*HP* 96). I can never sing the line 'Rise to adore the mystery of love' in the opening verse without being reminded that love, in all its forms and at every level of our experience, *is* a mystery to which adoration of its ultimate source ('We love, because he first loved us') is the least inadequate response. That is never more appropriate than at Christmas, which represents God's most tremendous pledge of his love to all the world – and me.

A personal favourite, this time from the 19th-century, is *HP* 98, 'Cradled in a manger, meanly', by George Stringer Rowe. Whether it is the only hymn he wrote I do not know, but he is deservedly remembered for this one alone. Yes, we have all the usual trimmings of the Christmas story, though in a restrained form without the glitterwax; and there is one line I can identify with only imperfectly at best: the suggestion that we should be sorry for those 'who have winter, but no Christmas' (v.4). On the only occasion when I found myself on more than a fleeting visit to a tropical country, where the only seasons were an alternation between monsoon and drought, I caught myself thinking, 'I could live without Christmas, but not without winter!' – but that, once again, is to beg the question as to what is implied by 'Christmas', which in Stringer Rowe's mind I am sure was the coming of what another traditional carol calls 'the truth sent from above'. So it is more to the point that in *HP* 98 we have what may be called an internalisation of the Nativity in the second half of vv2 and 3. Joined together, these lines make a meaningful prayer for this time of the year, culminating in the thought that heaven is, first and last, Christ's indwelling presence with us. *HP* 113 v.4 expresses the same thought in familiar words:

> Cast out our sin, and enter in;
> Be born in us today!

That in its way expresses the beginning and the end of the Christmas message.

But a carol does not have to be hoary with age and redolent with the past to be acceptable. Once again Timothy Dudley-Smith serves us well here. 'Child of the stable's secret birth' (*HP* 124) not only makes the humanity of the Christ child very real, but verse by verse links his birth with later aspects of his earthly life, suggesting more than enough material for a single sermon. Geoffrey Ainger's modern carol 'Mary's Child' (*HP* 95) has become an established favourite and its four verses can readily form the basis for a meditation on the significance of the one who was 'born in a borrowed room', yet has come to be recognised and hailed as the source of the world's light, truth and hope.

It would be a waste of breath, or printer's ink, to plead that we should leave out the Magi from our Christmas celebrations, so that they might come into their own at Epiphany, when we celebrate the 'manifestation' of Christ to the Gentile world. But even if neither you nor your congregation can bear yet another appearance on stage of the 'Three Wise Men', the Epiphany theme is too important to be ignored entirely. There is plenty of material in Charles Wesley's 'Stupendous height of heavenly love' (*HP* 462) to serve your purpose and to draw the Christmas season to a close with a resounding fanfare of trumpets. The light that Christ's coming has brought into the world (John 1:6-9) is referred to in every verse of the hymn and can be illustrated from countless examples through the centuries. There is surely no more tremendous opening line anywhere in Christian hymnody; and as for a text offering a breathtaking vista on human history and beyond, what is there that compares with the opening of v.4?

> Answer thy mercy's whole design,
>   My God incarnated for me.

7

PASSIONTIDE

Palm Sunday

It would be difficult to conduct worship on Palm Sunday without singing either 'Ride on, ride on in majesty!' (*HP* 159) or 'All glory, laud, and honour' (*HP* 160). In the latter case the compilers of *Hymns & Psalms*, whether out of a preference for Neale's original or to avoid undue repetition, have carried out major surgery which has left the patient gasping for breath. What they seem not to have noticed was that the real repetition was not in the refrain, but in the main body of the hymn, where the parallel between the shouts of the Palm Sunday crowd and our worship is repeated with minor variations no fewer than four times in vv2 and 3. For some reason I cannot quite pin down, the version most of us are familiar with (e.g. *MHB* 84) seems more effective and tolerable.

The one thing noticeably lacking in both these Palm Sunday hymns (and also in the much more pedestrian 'Children of Jerusalem' (*HP* 163)) is any recognition of the fact that those who cried 'Hosanna' outside Jerusalem had little if any understanding of the significant event they were witnessing. As his own disciples found, it is much easier to shout 'Hosanna!' than to follow Jesus all the way to Calvary. If the similarity between the Palm Sunday crowd and ourselves as modern worshippers had been brought out more fully in these hymns, this could make them more meaningful to us as we sing them. Are not *we* often 'slow of heart' and our praises sometimes uncomprehending?

That said, Milman's hymn (*HP* 159) has much to commend it. I leave for later comment the pregnant lines in v.2,

> O Christ, thy triumphs now begin
> O'er captive death and conquered sin,

apart from pointing out that a sermon based on that couplet could certainly be preached on other occasions besides Palm Sunday. A noticeable strength of the hymn is the cosmic dimensions of the way it views the 'triumphal entry' *sub specie aeternitatis*, notably in such phrases as 'the wingèd squadrons of the sky' (v.3) and the Father's 'sapphire throne' (v.4), even if the imagery is beginning to seem a little old-fashioned.

Hymns & Psalms has given us two more recent alternatives to these traditional hymns. The strength of *HP* 161, 'The glory of our King was seen', lies both in the simplicity of its language and in its progression, verse by verse, from Palm Sunday through Good Friday to Easter Day, Christ's glory being manifested not just by his resurrection, but on all three occasions. *HP* 162, 'Trotting, trotting through Jerusalem' makes up for the deficiency I have mentioned in *HP* 159 and 160 by noting the incomprehension of the Palm Sunday crowd, many of whom 'thought he should have come on a mighty horse, leading all the Jews to battle' and so 'were amazed to see such a quiet man trotting on a donkey'. This is the Eastertide equivalent of George MacDonald's nativity verse:

> They all were looking for a king
> To slay their foes, and lift them high;
> Thou cam'st, a little baby thing,
> That made a woman cry.

Chesterton's poem, 'The Donkey', might also be pressed into service here.

Good Friday

What is widely considered the greatest of all Good Friday hymns, Isaac Watts' 'When I survey the wondrous cross' (*HP* 180), has already been considered in another context. All that we need do here, perhaps, is to note how powerfully and effectively in verse after verse Watts maintains a double focus: on the death of Christ, combined with our human response to the crucified Lord. Charles Wesley falls far short of Watts at this point; when, as in *HP* 185 ('Would Jesus have the sinner die?'), he tries to achieve the same synthesis of the historical and the personal, he descends into what is, by comparison, morbid sentimentality. It could almost be said that the contrast between these two hymns epitomises the difference between classicism and romanticism. There is a warning here for any of us who attempt to preach on the crucifixion, as we all must surely do from time to time. The last thing we should knowingly do is to sentimentalise what was a hideously painful way of dying. Watts' emotional restraint should be our model.

No less a person than John Henry Newman lets us down at this focal point in our faith. You will know that memorably dismissive passage in Bernard Lord Manning's *The Hymns of Wesley and Watts*, where he berates Newman's 'mean conclusion' to his otherwise splendid hymn, 'Praise to the Holiest in the height' (*HP* 231). Newman declares that the *raison d'être* of Christ's passion is

> To teach his brethren, and inspire
> To suffer and to die.

Surprisingly, in view of the other editorial 'improvements', this anticlimax has not been omitted or replaced in *Hymns & Psalms*. Fortunately, we can avoid Newman's 'humanitarian tinkling', since the wealth of Passiontide hymns at our disposal amounts almost to an embarrassment of riches. One way to pick our way through them may be to consider the main ways in which the question 'How can the death of Christ in first-century Palestine possibly have any effect on our life in the present?' has been answered over the centuries. In other words, we can look at how these hymns reflect the different 'theories of the atonement', bearing in mind that these are no more than metaphors which attempt to express the significance of the crucifixion.

One of the earliest of these is the idea that Christ's death was a 'ransom', the price he paid to free us from enslavement or imprisonment, echoing the words of Jesus himself recorded in Mark 10:45.

It is as well to steer well clear of the pitfall of asking (as some early Christian theologians did) to whom the ransom was paid, which risks stretching the metaphor to breaking-point. It is enough to say, with a modern hymn like *HP* 260, that he 'gave his life a ransom, thus setting us free'.

Charles Wesley picks up the idea almost in passing and gives us a resounding opening to *HP* 440:

> Omnipotent Redeemer,
>> Our ransomed souls adore thee;

in *HP* 168 he writes:

> He has our salvation wrought,
> He our captive souls has bought;

and in *HP* 175 he pleads with us to

> Believe, believe the record true,
>> We all are bought with Jesu's blood.

In *HP* 178 Mrs Alexander couches it in simpler language:

> There was no other good enough
>> To pay the price of sin,

though she falls from grace in the second half of the same verse by seeming to assert that the 'gate of heaven' was locked and barred against us until Christ unlocked it; as though God had kept the gates firmly closed until that moment! (Her words always remind me of that chorus in Stainer's *Crucifixion* in which 'Fling wide the gates!' is repeated with such tedious persistence that one begins to wonder whether the archangels on duty have not fallen asleep at their post.) A similar problem arises in lines from a splendid Easter hymn (*HP* 214):

> He broke the age-bound chains of hell;
> The bars from heaven's high portals fell. (v.4)

When we have made full allowance for the figurative nature of the language, we still need to ask, 'Does it convey quite the wrong image to 21st-century minds?' In reinstating a verse omitted from *MHB* 215, the compilers of *Hymns & Psalms* must have concluded that it doesn't, but I am not so sure. Much nearer the mark, to my mind, is the imagery in C S Lewis's *The Great Divorce*, an allegory which depicts the entrance to heaven as wide open for anyone who chooses to enter, so that we debar ourselves from heaven only by our preference for the dreariness of hell. That does not remove the element of divine judgement, but relocates it to where it seems to me to be more meaningful.

Secondly, there is the concept of Jesus as our 'substitute'; that in some way he 'took our place' and paid the price of our sin by suffering a punishment that should by rights have been ours. This was no doubt more easily accepted in the days when a prince might have among his entourage a companion who was his 'whipping boy', to receive the chastisement which would otherwise be due to his royal master for his misdemeanours. Our sense of justice has, at least in some respects, developed since those days, so that the idea of substitution is less helpful to us as we strive to understand why Jesus needed to die on the cross. Yet it is not by any means entirely played out, if only because it is a fact of life that people often suffer the consequences of the shortcomings of others. Furthermore, there is a closely related idea which surfaces in many of these hymns: that we, for our sins, *deserve* to suffer what Jesus in his innocence did not at all deserve. Once we have transferred the underlying idea from the setting of a court of law to that of personal relationships, it takes on a quite new validity.

However, unless we are careful to avoid setting his love and his justice at odds, we risk proclaiming a less than Christian concept of God. Mrs Clephane hovers perilously close to the pitfall when she describes the cross as a

> trysting-place where heaven's love
> And heaven's justice meet! (*HP* 165 v.2)

On the other hand, to see how much virtue the 'substitutionary theory' still retains we have only to remember Robert Bridges' translation of a German penitential hymn, 'Ah, holy Jesus, how hast thou offended' (*HP* 164), with its moving second verse:

> Who was the guilty? Who brought this upon thee?
> Alas, my treason, Jesus, hath undone thee.
> Twas I, Lord Jesus, I it was denied thee:
>   I crucified thee.

Taken literally, such language would be manifest nonsense; we were *not* there and so had nothing to do with his execution. Why should we be blamed, any more than Britishers at the beginning of the 21st-century should be held responsible for their 18th-century forefathers' involvement in the brutalities of the slave trade? Or modern Catholics be tarred with the fanatical excesses of the Inquisition? We have at last, let us hope, cast off the centuries of Christian anti-Semitism which held each succeeding generation of Jews guilty of having crucified the Son of God. Isn't it time that the underlying idea of retrospective guilt was abandoned altogether?

But it is as well to pause a moment, long enough at least to ask whether there is not a true insight in the verse just quoted? What could more powerfully express our failure to be worthy of what Samuel Crossman calls Christ's 'love to the loveless shown, that they might lovely be'? Though we hardly believe it in our habitual, day-to-day state of mind, in moments of really searching self-appraisal we may come to recognise that it is we, not Christ, who deserve whatever penalties are going. Or, to put it in a slightly more moderate way, and to quote Crossman again:

> In life no house, no home,
>> My Lord on earth might have;
> In death no friendly tomb
>> But what a stranger gave.
>>> What may I say?
>>>> Heaven was his home;
>>>> But mine the tomb
>>> Wherein he lay. (*HP* 173 v.6)

This theme of Christ taking our place and suffering for our sake crops up frequently:

> Thou, O my Jesus, thou didst me
>> Upon the cross embrace;
> For me didst bear the nails and spear,
>> And manifold disgrace. (*HP* 171 v.2)

> The Father's co-eternal Son
>> Bore all my sins upon the tree; (*HP* 175 v.1)

and in that deeply felt expression of Christ's passion, the German 'O sacred Head, sore wounded' (*HP* 176):

> Thy grief and thy compassion
>> Were all for sinners' gain;
> Mine, mine was the transgression,
>> But thine the deadly pain. (v.2)

It is certainly necessary to handle this idea of 'substitution' carefully, lest we give the impression that God needed to punish *someone*, whether to appease his anger or satisfy his 'honour', and picked on the first willing victim to show up. (I put this crudely, because all too often this 'substitutionary' theory of the atonement has been couched in similarly crude language.) But the language of devotion, including that of the hymn-writers, has done more, I suggest, to make it acceptable and meaningful than any amount of theological debate.

A different interpretation of Christ's atoning death is that of a decisive victory over evil. This too has been around for many centuries, but in more recent times was given a new lease of life by Gustaf Aulén in his influential book *Christus Victor* (1931). As an alternative to thinking of the resurrection as Christ's victory over death, a turning of the tables on his enemies, here is a way of viewing it which encourages us to look deeper than the surface events of Good Friday. Christ's victory was one of 'obedience even unto death' and of 'love triumphant still in death' (*HP* 183 v.4) – a victory won not by his rising again, but by the 'anguish' and 'faith' demonstrated on Calvary. Notice, similarly, how the context of Pratt Green's declaration in *HP* 186 v.2 that 'Love has overcome' is not Easter morning, but Good Friday evening, as Jesus is laid in the tomb. Indeed, Milman's Palm Sunday hymn, which we have noted above, declares that the victory began even earlier than Good Friday:

> O Christ, thy triumphs now begin
> O'er captive death and conquered sin. (*HP* 159 v.2)

The effect of this is only slightly marred by the closing lines of the hymn, which make a *contrast* between the 'mortal pain' of Calvary and Christ's reigning in power (which presumably we are to envisage as following his resurrection).

An early expression of the idea of Jesus 'reigning from the cross' appears in Percy Dearmer's translation of one of the Church's ancient hymns ('Sing, my tongue, the glorious battle', *HP* 177), where the 'faithful cross' (presumably, 'the cross on which Jesus kept faith with God' by his obedience) is itself a 'sign of triumph' (v.4). But it is more fully worked out in later hymns, such as M R Newbolt's 'Lift high the cross' (*HP* 170), where the triumphant celebration does not have to wait for Easter morning to dawn. His resurrection sets the seal on this victory, but it is a victory already won. This point is missed in a couplet from Doreen Newport's 'Think of a world' (*HP* 572), where she invites us in verse 7 to

> Think of a cross without a resurrection,
> Only a grave and not a victory won.

'*Only* a grave'? There is just enough ambiguity in the second line taken in isolation for it just possibly to pass the litmus test, but in parallel with the previous one the implication that the cross was a defeat which had to be reversed is inescapable.

The early Church found it natural to think of Christ's death as a cosmic victory over the Devil, breaking his hold over human nature. Such language comes less naturally to us, though the reality of evil, whether personified or not, is if anything more inescapable than ever in our world. But there is a modern equivalent at our disposal. At the personal level, Charles Wesley was in no doubt of the possibility of our victory over sin because of what Christ has achieved (*HP* 168, especially vv3-5). As Mrs Alexander put it, in commendably simple words, 'He died to make us good' (*HP* 178 v.3), i.e. not just to gain forgiveness for us, but to *change* us. And this is echoed in many hymns that do not belong specifically to this season. One hymn, however, which fails at this point is *HP* 167, 'In the cross of Christ I glory', where amidst all the blessings enumerated there is no hint of 'sins forgiven'. The sanctifying of 'bane and blessing, pain and pleasure' (v.4) is, we might say, no more than a secondary benefit by comparison.

Rather surprisingly, the word 'sacrifice' rarely seems to occur in connection with the crucifixion, though the *idea* is often lurking somewhere in the background, e.g. in references to the blood of Christ. For the fullest treatment of this theme we have to look in the section of *Hymns & Psalms* on the Lord's Supper, where *HP* 629 is addressed to the 'Victim divine . . . once offered up a spotless Lamb' to atone for 'all mankind'. Here, especially in v.2, Old Testament sacrificial ritual is interpreted in New Testament terms, chiefly in the Epistle to the Hebrews. This is the only one of the hymns in Charles Wesley's *Hymns on the Lord's Supper* (from the section called 'The Holy Eucharist as it implies a Sacrifice') to have found a place in present-day worship. Hebrews is also the background for the closing lines of William Chatterton Dix's 'Alleluia! Sing to Jesus' (*HP* 592):

> Thou within the veil hast entered,
>> Robed in flesh, our great High Priest;
> Thou on earth both priest and victim
>> In the eucharistic feast.

If Dix's language here seems too High Church for your taste (and I myself would certainly want to object to Christ's priestly role being confined to or even focused in the Eucharist), perhaps it is because you have not studied Hebrews recently (we all tend to be selective in our Bible reading). Hebrews spells out in detail the parallel between the sacrificial ritual of the Temple in Jerusalem, with its human limitations, and the one perfect sacrifice of Christ, which is the supreme act of *self*-sacrifice. Dix's hymn would be a good way of helping a congregation to get to the heart of a New Testament book which is widely neglected because its thought world is both complex and far removed from our own as 21st-century Christians.

'Lord Christ, we praise your sacrifice' (*HP* 532) is another modern hymn which explores this theme, describing Christ's sacrifice as his 'life in love so freely given'. Again, the hymn is all the more meaningful because it does not separate his death from the rest of his life, but sees both as part of that 'willing helplessness' which we are called upon to share (v.4). Here again the crucifixion itself is seen as a victory, through which 'God's eternal love' is 'proclaimed'.

One way of approaching any of the gospel stories is to imagine oneself present as a spectator or participant. A number of the Passiontide hymns do this in passing, but the best example is the American spiritual, 'Were you there when they crucified my Lord?' (*HP* 181). Like the Roman Catholic 'stations of the cross', this focuses on a sequence of events, though in this case reaching its climax with the resurrection. Its effect lies in its simplicity and firmly controlled emotion. But although the four-verse structure provides an obvious framework for a sermon, I am not sure that any elaboration of its message could do more than lessen the impact of the hymn itself. There are times, even for preachers, when to keep silent is more meaningful than any speech.

'Were you there?' might perhaps be classed as an example of yet another 'theory of the atonement'. The 'moral influence' theory has a pedigree going back at least to Peter Abelard, the influential but controversial theologian of the 12th century mainly remembered for his love affair with Heloise. But it has had a mixed press. It has its modern advocates among those who find some of the more traditional atonement theories outmoded and unacceptable. Others have dismissed it as too 'subjective'. In essence, it interprets the influence of the crucifixion in terms of its power to shame us into penitence and obedience. Assuming such changes in us to be genuine and lasting, I am not clear why they should be considered less 'objective' than a metaphorical victory over Satan or the payment of an equally metaphorical 'ransom' to an unspecified party. It seems to be assumed that 'subjective' implies 'unreal' or 'imaginary', whereas the 'objective' events are real because they occur in the outside world and independently of our involvement in them. This surely needs to be challenged. What Charles Wesley is describing in *HP* 185 ('Would Jesus have the sinner die?') is unmistakably a change 'within' us, and therefore subjective; but it is surely no less real for that when it does occur. To take a parallel case: if we reject the claim that the validity of the Sacrament depends on an objective change in the elements of bread and wine (i.e. transubstantiation), should we not find it possible to accept that the effect of Christ's death on our hearts and minds is no less real for being 'subjective'?

At any rate, it is heartening, and by no means surprising, to find many echoes of this understanding of the crucifixion in the devotional literature of the hymn book. Hymn after hymn gives expression to the gamut of responses to the cross, moving from sorrow, through shame and wonder to gratitude and love. The overall theme of Charles Wesley's 'God of unexampled grace' (*HP* 166) is the thought that it is God himself who is crucified on our behalf; but the emphasis throughout is on our response, through praise, wonder and faith in successive verses. *HP* 171, 'My God, I love thee' is based on the words of 1 John 4:19, 'We love, because he first loved us', and declares that such love as his, and only that, can achieve in us what neither hope of heaven nor fear of hell can inspire. For further examples, look up *HP* 183, 184 (especially vv4 and 5), and above all 'When I survey the wondrous cross' (*HP* 180) which we have already considered.

8

EASTERTIDE

R esurrection

My own short list of those hymns without which Easter Day would be incomplete includes:

> Good Christians all, rejoice and sing! (*HP* 191)
> Christ the Lord is risen again! (*HP* 192)
> Christ the Lord is risen today (*HP* 193)
> The day of resurrection (*HP* 208)

Such hymns as these enable us to celebrate the joy of Christ's resurrection. If they do so without necessarily offering us food for thought, so be it. They are no less a part of the high tradition of Christian worship. The gospel records themselves raise plenty of questions to exercise our minds, while our hearts are rejoicing and our lives responding to the Easter event. But this season's hymns also have a part to play as we grapple with what we may well claim to be the greatest event in history.

As with Christmas, though to a much lesser extent, Christian and pagan traditions are intermingled in the celebration of Easter. According to Bede, the name itself derives from a pagan spring goddess, Eostre. The giving of Easter eggs, as a symbol of new life and not just of a sweet tooth, is also very ancient. So it is not surprising to find Easter hymns which associate the resurrection with the springtime renewal of life. Before we dismiss this as merely residual paganism, we should remember how prominently the natural world features in the parables of Jesus. C S Lewis, answering the charge that Christianity was no more than a reworking of pagan myths, used to argue the contrary view that those myths were themselves an imperfect foreshadowing of the truth only fully revealed in Christ. In much the same way, we could say that Easter customs that can be traced to pagan origins may nevertheless embody insights, derived from the renewal of life in spring, which find their fulfilment in Christ's rising again.

The ancient Israelites were understandably apprehensive about the insidious influence of Canaanite fertility rites, which, as the Old Testament shows, were a serious temptation to the nomadic tribes whose sterner faith derived from a God of the desert. The creation stories in Genesis and references in the Psalms and the book of Isaiah to God active in the natural world were probably part of the counter-propaganda. That Israelite apprehension was inherited by Christianity. But the God of history is also the God of nature, so that not just at harvest time, but here at Easter there is a place for these references to the natural world. As one of the early Christian hymns puts it:

> Let all things *seen* and *unseen*
> Their notes of gladness blend. (*HP* 208 v.3)

More explicitly, the opening verse of *HP* 186 sets the resurrection of Jesus and the spring season side by side:

> After darkness, light;
> After winter, spring;
> After dying, life:
> Alleluia!

But the parallel is drawn out most fully in the hauntingly beautiful 'Now the green blade rises from the buried grain' (*HP* 204), where the renewal of life in nature serves as a parable not only of the historical resurrection, but of the renewal of our spiritual life in Christ:

> When our hearts are wintry, grieving, or in pain,
> Then your touch can call us back to life again,
> Fields of our hearts that dead and bare have been:
> *Love is come again, like wheat that springs up green.*

The hymn is based on John 12:24, where Jesus is speaking of his own death and resurrection: 'Except a grain of wheat fall into the earth and die, it abideth by itself alone: but if it die, it beareth much fruit' (AV). But it is also a modern reworking of Paul's great theme in 1 Corinthians 15:36-38, where the apostle uses the same analogy to describe *our* spiritual renewal or rebirth. When love of nature is mentioned in the pulpit, it is quite often dismissed as 'nature worship', the 'natural' person's substitute for genuine religion – or an excuse for not 'going to church'. But here in the New Testament we find a more positive attitude, showing that our appreciation of natural beauty, whether out in the countryside or through the arts, can be not only good in itself, but a pointer to greater and deeper things of the spirit, as in several of Gerard Manley Hopkins' poems.

All the same, we are justified in having reservations about our response to nature, which can readily lapse into pantheism. The safeguard is to distinguish clearly between the beauty of the created world and its Creator, whom we celebrate at Easter as 'the Lord of Life' who 'is risen for aye' (*HP* 191 v.2). To him, and only to him, is it appropriate to bring 'flowers of song to strew his way'. Whether or not this is meant to hark back to the Triumphal Entry I do not know; but it is surely a deliberate echo of George Herbert's poem 'Easter':

> I got me flowers to strew thy way
> I got me boughs off many a tree;
> But thou wast up by break of day,
> And brought'st thy sweets along with thee.

Isaac Watts makes the essential distinction between Creator and creation in *HP* 24 v.2:

Thy voice produced the sea and spheres,
  Bade the waves roar, the planets shine;
But nothing like thyself appears
  Through all these spacious works of thine.

So let us by all means both enjoy and use the natural world in a way that shows our awareness of its Creator. (We shall return to this topic in Chapter 10.)

Our celebration of Christ's triumph at Calvary is rightly and properly muted until Easter Day dawns, when we can begin to share the wonder and joy of the first disciples at the news that 'He is risen indeed!' Easter then sets the seal on the victory already won and initiates our proclamation to the world that evil can never ultimately triumph, since

Easter makes it plain
His kingdom is not shaken. (*HP* 213 v.2)

Not that a facile optimism can be justified in view of the kind of world we live in. In this respect, *HP* 187, 'Away with gloom, away with doubt!', which the authors of the *Companion to Hymns & Psalms* describe as 'deservedly popular', seems to me the least acceptable of Easter hymns. Despite the biblical allusions in verse 1, much of its imagery is secular and vague; and I can only excuse the line 'And welcome peace, away with strife!' on the grounds that Shillito was writing in the aftermath of the 'Great War' (the hymn was first published in 1919) and shared the relief and euphoria of the time. We have learned from hard experience that it is not that simple and that however justifiably we may hail Christ as 'Prince of peace', it is *not* because 'he maketh wars to cease unto the end of the earth' (Psalm 46:9 AV). If we are going to persuade our contemporaries to give serious consideration to the claims of Christianity, we shall have to do much better than that.

If Good Friday should be interpreted in the light of Easter Day, the complementary truth is that the meaning of the resurrection is only to be understood against the background of Calvary. Brian Wren's 'Christ is alive!' (*HP* 190) brings this out in a single line:

> His love in death shall never die.

I cannot think of any other hymn which offers a more powerful text in our present world for a sermon on the resurrection. Verses 3 and 4 of the hymn spell out the implications of this line. The risen Christ lives and reigns to all eternity, but not in some remote heavenly splendour, 'untouched, unmoved by human pains'. Rather, by the very fact that he is alive, he continues to share in the world's suffering:

> In every insult, rift and war,
>> Where colour, scorn or wealth divide.

More boldly than in any of the traditional Easter hymns, Wren declares that Christ 'lives, though ever crucified' (v.4). We have come a long way from the days when Patripassianism was dismissed as a heresy. In similar vein, *HP* 191 proclaims a God, both crucified and risen, who is so far from being indifferent to the world's suffering that he enters into and shares it with us.

The impossibility of separating Easter from Good Friday is nowhere more clearly shown than in Thomas Kelly's 'The head that once was crowned with thorns' (*HP* 209), and notably in v.4 and again in v.6:

> The cross he bore is life and health,
>> Though shame and death to him;
> His people's hope, his people's wealth,
>> Their everlasting theme.

Either the antithesis and chiasmus of lines 1 and 2, or the piling up of the blessings that are ours through his cross in the final couplet could quite appropriately be explored in an Easter sermon.

If there is one note missing in this hymn, it is the one struck by Charles Wesley in *HP* 188: 'His rise proclaims your sins forgiven' (v.2), and this omission is even more blatant in both 'I know that my Redeemer lives' (*HP* 196) and 'Jesus lives!' (*HP* 198), each of which catalogues and celebrates the blessings that are ours through Christ's resurrection: assurance of his love, freedom from fear of death, confident anticipation of heaven, and so on – all far from negligible blessings indeed. All the more curious, therefore, that there is no mention of our present relief from the burden of sin, unless we find it hinted at in the line, 'He lives to plead for me above' (*HP* 196 v.2). Wesley is, by contrast, in no doubt of our *present* benefit from the resurrection:

> Go, tell the followers of your Lord
> Their Jesus is to life restored;
> He lives, that they his life may find. (*HP* 188 v.4)

So the blessings which are ours here and now through our risen Lord are not confined to forgiveness, but amount to a new life in him. An Easter hymn by G W Briggs (*HP* 203) begins boldly and in similar vein with the assertion that

> *Now* is eternal life,
> If risen with Christ we stand.

The fourth verse spells out this Pauline claim:

> Unfathomed love divine,
> Reign thou within my heart;
> From thee nor depth nor height,
> Nor life nor death can part;
> My life is hid in God with thee,
> Now and through all eternity.

This is a working out of one of Charles Wesley's favourite themes, of 'heaven begun below'. It carries us well beyond the euphoria of Easter Day to the challenge of living out our faith in the risen Christ day by day.

If you are looking, not just for a text, but for an Easter sermon outline, what about *HP* 206 v.4?

The Lord, that all his foes o'ercame,
The world, sin, death, and hell o'erthrew;
And Jesus is the conqueror's name.

Is there significance in the order of the words in that second line, or are they determined merely by literary considerations? I *think* I detect a logical progression. As a preacher, I might do worse than stop talking for five minutes and ask my congregation to work this out for themselves. (I might even give out pencils and paper, but that might reveal the schoolteacher in me!)

Ascension

In *Hymns & Psalms* the Ascension is subsumed under the same heading as the Resurrection; understandably so, not just because, falling on a weekday, Ascension Day is largely neglected, but because the two events are closely associated. The biblical imagery is here conspicuously at odds with the heliocentric solar system familiar to us through modern science. To some extent traditional imagery can survive alongside our scientific knowledge: we have no difficulty in speaking of 'sunrise' and 'sunset'. But in the case of the Ascension there is more at stake than a convenient figure of speech. When a Russian astronaut, returning safely to earth, reports (to all appearances, quite seriously) that he found no evidence of heaven 'up there', it is surely time to abandon the imagery associated with the 'three-decker universe' of biblical times, however difficult it may be to find workable substitutes.

The relevance of this to our present topic lies in the need for us, as preachers, to help our congregations reinterpret the traditional language and not be misled by it. The essential truth expressed in Luke's account of the Ascension is Christ's continuing presence, not his absence in heaven; and that presence is no longer physical and therefore localised, but ubiquitous. Hence passages such as Matthew 28:20 and John 14:18 and 23. Language that a pre-Copernican age found natural and meaningful is no longer helpful. Indeed, unless used with care, it never was; witness the once popular gospel hymn which declared:

> He will come back one day
> From his home *far away*.

Charles Wesley is still working in the old imagery in his glorious Ascensiontide hymn, 'Hail the day that sees him rise' (*HP* 197) and we would be impoverishing ourselves if we abandoned it in an access of modernity. But a verse like

> Master, parted from our sight,
> High above yon azure height,
> Grant our hearts may thither rise,
> Following thee *beyond the skies:* (v.5)

calls for some demythologising, as do phrases like 'above the sky' (*HP* 189 v.4).

At best, the spatial imagery expresses our awareness of a multidimensional universe, of planes of reality that are different but interconnected, rather than the blinkered vision of the modern materialist. So 'up there' is one way of expressing a conviction that there are 'higher' levels of reality and existence than the purely physical. If this seems too obvious to need spelling out to a modern congregation, remember the response to John Robinson's paperback, *Honest to God* as recently as 1963, in which he dared to question a literal 'ascension', along with other traditional expressions of Christian truth. Perhaps Christians have gone some way since then towards 'coming of age' in understanding their faith in the light of contemporary knowledge; but it would be hazardous to assume that there is no educational and pastoral task still to be done among our congregations. After all, if God is not 'up there', where is he?

9

PENTECOST

The Holy Spirit

The Holy Spirit is not the easiest Person of the Trinity to describe or preach about. The images most often used to represent 'him' – fire, wind, dove – are more obviously symbolic than those of Fatherhood, Kingship and so on; at the same time they may inadvertently encourage us to slip into impersonal language, referring to the Spirit as 'it' rather than 'he' or 'she'. Some of the hymns in the section of *Hymns & Psalms* entitled 'The Eternal Spirit' can help us focus on the *personal* nature of the third Person of the Trinity, and some of them are helpfully structured from the preacher's point of view, since they deal, verse by verse, with various aspects of the Spirit's work in us:

> Gracious Spirit, dwell with me (*HP* 286)
> Holy Spirit, come, confirm us (*HP* 288)
> Holy Spirit, truth divine (*HP* 289)
> Spirit of God within me (*HP* 294)

Any one of these could readily become a sermon outline. *HP* 294 explores different ways in which God may 'possess' us if we open ourselves to his presence: at the level of our human bodies and the human nature inextricably tied up with them (v.1); at the level of intellect which, like the physical eye, is blind apart from the light which enables it to see and understand (v.2); at the level of our loving response to others without which we cannot claim to love God (v.3). Finally, v.4 challenges us, like

HP 288, to be possessed wholly by God's Spirit – not just our physical and intellectual faculties, but we ourselves, so that, finite creatures that we are, we may eventually transcend the limitations of our earthly existence. This is a spiritual dimension of our hope in Christ that we do not often spell out in these earthbound days, but it is part of the hope that is ours as Christ's redeemed.

The three verses of *HP* 309, 'O God, O Spirit known to us', speak of different ways in which the God who is, by his very nature, ineffable, can nevertheless be known to us – through the created universe, through Christ's earthly life and through the Spirit at work in the lives of others (prompting the thought that we do not make anything like enough of Christian biography in our preaching).

The last three verses of Charles Wesley's 'My God, I know, I feel thee mine' (*HP* 740) focus on a quite different aspect of the Spirit's work as a 'refining fire' which purges the dross of our sin. We may find ourselves less at ease with this than with the more gentle images of breath or dove, but that could be a measure of our need of it as a corrective to ideas of God the Holy Spirit that are too cosy. Both images, of fire and dove, are found in *HP* 129 v.1, though in a rather subdued form; and I am not quite sure what an 'urgent' flame is.

The other hymns I have listed above invite us to explore different aspects of the Spirit's work in our hearts and in our daily lives. *HP* 288 is based on some of the words of Jesus in the upper room on the eve of his arrest and crucifixion; in particular on his references to the 'Advocate' (or 'Comforter' or 'Counsellor') whom he promises to send to his disciples after he is taken from them. John 14:26 explicitly identifies this promised gift of the 'Paraclete' with the Holy Spirit, so that the promise is fulfilled at Pentecost. (In 1 John 2:1, the only use of the word elsewhere in the New Testament, it refers to Jesus himself.) From among the various shades of meaning discernible in the Greek word 'Paraclete', *HP* 288 focuses on that of 'Advocate', but the alternatives are not entirely absent. So in v.1 we pray that he will 'confirm us in the truth that Christ makes known', ie. that he will guide us into a deeper understanding of Christ's teaching, which is by no means as simple or as readily acceptable as we sometimes persuade ourselves. In v.2 the word 'Advocate' itself is used. 'Paraclete' can be translated literally as 'one who stands at our side' and so reassures and strengthens us by giving us 'the help we need'. The last two verses invite us to a deeper understanding of the presence of God's Spirit outwardly in our lives (v.3) and inwardly in our hearts (v.4). From his being 'at our side' and accompanying us on life's journey, we are encouraged to see as the goal of discipleship a closer union with God himself, reflecting the unity of the Godhead with which the hymn ends.

It ought to be the case that the Holy Spirit, who is God as we encounter him in our everyday lives, is more real to us than the Father or the Son. In practice, unless we are Pentecostalists, he (or she) is likely to seem the most ethereal and even 'ghostly' member of the Godhead. And even among Charismatics the emphasis tends to be on such extraordinary gifts as 'speaking in tongues', whereas the New Testament focuses more on the enhancement of what we might call 'natural' gifts.

Several hymns refer to the Spirit's 'sevenfold gifts'; e.g. *HP* 283:

> Thou the anointing Spirit art,
> Who dost thy sevenfold gifts impart (v.1)

with which we may compare *HP* 284 v.5; 302 v.2; 337 v.5. 'Sevenfold' occurs a number of times in the Old Testament, referring to abundance of some sort; the nearest New Testament equivalent being the occasion when Peter asks Jesus how often he must forgive his brother (Matthew 18:21). There are also the 'seven Spirits' which occur in Revelation 1:4 and elsewhere, but these are as puzzling (and possibly heretical!) as much else in that book. We may be on safer ground if we note that Christian tradition identifies Isaiah 11:2 as the origin of the phrase. It is difficult to take this as more than a rather desperate attempt to find scriptural support for what may be no more than the use of seven as the 'ideal' number. For one thing, the Isaiah passage mentions, at most, only six 'gifts of the spirit'. More importantly, the prophet is speaking of a future descendant of King David ('a shoot out of the stump of Jesse') who would inaugurate an age of justice and peace. We can apply this to our own spiritual experience only by stretching the similarity to breaking point.

We are on much firmer ground if we look to a New Testament passage such as 1 Corinthians 12:4-10, where no fewer than *nine* 'gifts of the Spirit' are listed. (If the exact number seems important or significant to you, some doubling up is possible to reduce the total to seven; but do not lose sight of Paul's main theme in your enthusiasm for the arithmetic!) It is surely justifiable in this case to focus our attention on the gifts rather than on the Giver, provided we do not lose sight of the fact that they *are* his gifts, not our own unaided abilities. (The 'talents' in the parable, Matthew 25:14-30, were, after all, given, or rather *lent*, to the servants, to be *used* in their lord's service.) In other words, if we want to recognise the Holy Spirit, we will do best to look at the effect he has on us and our lives.

Although in *HP* 320 Pratt Green speaks of 'the Spirit's gifts to me', the hymn is actually based on what Paul says about the *fruits* of the Spirit in Galatians 5:22, where he places 'love, joy and peace' at the head of the list. In calling them 'fruits' he is emphasising that they are not natural states of mind, but the result of our opening our hearts and lives to the Spirit. It is worth dwelling on our experience of their opposites as a background to what the hymn has to say about each of these 'fruits' in verses 2-4. And the closing verse offers an application for our daily living. Timothy Dudley-Smith's meditation on Romans 8 in *HP* 279, 'Born by the Holy Spirit's breath', dwells on what the Spirit enables us to be and to do beyond our 'natural' abilities. We might think of the Spirit's work in terms of a kind of spiritual adrenalin, but if you are more attracted to the arts than to sport, then the inspiration of the creative artist may provide a better analogy.

HP 280 provides a possible text for a sermon stressing that the Spirit's influence is both 'internal' (on our hearts and minds) and 'external' (on our lives and actions):

> Breathe on me, Breath of God, . . .
> That I may love what thou dost love,
> And do what thou wouldst do.

There are complementary truths to be emphasised here. The proof of the indwelling Spirit lies in actions, not feelings alone, but our actions in turn stem from what we are through the Spirit's influence. The much loved 'Come down, O Love divine' (*HP* 281) is mainly concerned with the *inward* effects of the Spirit, but verse 3 at least glances at his outward manifestation.

There is a crucial difference between being influenced by another person and losing one's own identity, e.g. through some form of brainwashing. Verse 3 of Charles Wesley's 'Come, Holy Ghost, all-quickening fire' (*HP* 282) comes dangerously close to suggesting the latter as a result of the indwelling Spirit. It is quite surprising that, in including this hymn in his 1780 hymn book, John Wesley allowed the lines

> Plunged in the Godhead's deepest sea,
> And lost in thine immensity

to stand, despite their closeness to the mysticism which he had come to distrust. To us, it may seem more reminiscent of the Buddhist goal of Nirvana. We have to ask, in experiencing the 'Spirit of the living God', do we lose our identity, or find it enhanced? Are we more, or less, our true selves when we fall head-over-heels in love? (Remember Housman's 'Shropshire lad' who fell in love and then out again, so that

> Miles around they'll say that I
> Am quite myself again.)

This same issue arises rather more forcefully in two lines from *HP* 295:

> Break me, melt me,
> Mould me, fill me . . .

This seems to invite a pretty devastating spiritual invasion of one's psyche. In my experience, perfectly sober, not to say eminently respectable, congregations sing these words with an unhesitating fervour that suggests they have not even begun to consider their meaning. (Perhaps it is as well that God does not always take us at our word!) Should we not more often challenge them to question the meaning of what we invite them to sing and be sure that they mean it, or at the very least, *want* to mean it?

HP 282 has more to offer, however, than a questionable hint of mystical self-annihilation. The closing couplet of v.4, with its echoes of 2 Corinthians 1:22 and Ephesians 1:13-14, cries out to be made the basis of a three-point sermon on what the Holy Spirit does for us:

> Seal of my sins in Christ forgiven,
> Earnest of love, and pledge of heaven.

And v.5 offers a view of the work of the Spirit in us that is dynamic, not static, and progressive, not instantaneous. We need not only to receive grace, but to grow in it.

Like other hymns associated with Pentecost, 'I want the Spir't of power within' (*HP* 291) is a hymn of aspiration, rather than of achievement, a case once again of our reach exceeding our grasp. This should make it particularly suitable for the 'average congregation'; but if Charles Wesley's words seem too strong meat for them, the first two verses of 'Spirit of God, descend upon my heart' (*HP* 313) may serve the same purpose:

I ask no dream, no prophet-ecstasies,
　　No sudden rending of the veil of clay,
No angel-visitant, no opening skies;
　　But take the dimness of my soul away.

We are 'dull of soul' indeed if we cannot pray those words!

Finally, at the heart of *HP* 290, a hymn that speaks of the Holy Spirit both as the agent of creation and the inspiration of the dispirited Apostles at the first Pentecost, Ann Phillips includes a telling reminder that he came, and still comes, 'through doors we close'. There are many ways in which this can be applied, which you will be able to work out for yourself – and for your hearers.

The Trinity

Perhaps it is a blessing that you will rarely hear a preacher on Trinity Sunday, one week after Pentecost, attempting to expound the orthodox Christian teaching on the triune God. To confuse the Persons of the Trinity is, of course (and I use the word advisedly) damnably heretical, deserving of the fires of Smithfield, since we have it on no less an authority than the so-called Athanasian Creed that we must neither 'confound the Persons', nor 'divide the Substance' of the Godhead, and the penalty for doing so is clearly spelled out! But take heart! If orthodox belief really *were* the essential condition of salvation, I fear that a good many of us would have little to hope for. But as we read the Bible, it is difficult to avoid the conclusion that there is a convergence, amounting at times to an overlap, in what is said about the risen Christ and about the Holy Spirit. How does Jesus' promise to be with his disciples 'even to the end of the world' differ from the presence of the Holy Spirit? Similarly, as we have already noted, both Jesus and the Spirit are described in the New Testament as the 'Paraclete' or Advocate. When it comes to creation, while God the Father is identified in the Creed as 'maker of heaven and earth', elsewhere both Son and Spirit are credited with being the agent (so perhaps it is permissible to confuse their functions, so long as we are clear about their Persons?).

Hymns reflect all this in the language they use. In *HP* 79 and *HP* 260 it is Jesus Christ by (or through) whom the universe was created. In *HP* 285 and *HP* 290 it is the Holy Spirit. Most of what is said about the continuing presence of Christ could be paralleled by references to the Spirit. Verse 1 of *HP* 289, 'Holy Spirit, truth divine', actually speaks of the Spirit as the 'Word of God', though that is a title reserved for Christ in the New Testament.

Whatever theologians may make of all this, to most of the congregation theorising about God the Holy Trinity must seem largely meaningless. Perhaps the most useful service we can render them is to help them realise that, like *all* the words and images we use to describe God, trinitarian language is necessarily metaphorical – at best, a pointer in the right direction. It is surely the simple truth that our God is still 'too small', even when we have clothed him in the trappings of trinitarian doctrine. To lose sight of this is potentially blasphemous in its apparent claim that the human mind can fully comprehend the nature of the Godhead.

All this may be of little consequence, but could be of some value if it alerts us to the limitations of human minds and human language when confronted with the divine ineffability. That is the only theme I find I can preach on Trinity Sunday, and a hymn like 'Immortal, invisible, God only wise' (*HP* 9) or 'How shall I sing that majesty' (*HP* 8) speaks more aptly than even 'Holy, holy, holy . . . God in three Persons, blessed Trinity' (*HP* 7). Attempts to enlist more orthodox trinitarian terminology have been conspicuously unsuccessful, whether by Charles Wesley, as in *HP* 6:

> Supreme, essential One, adored
> In co-eternal Three,

or in Newman's unbelievably flat-footed:

Firmly I believe and truly
God is Three and God is One;
and I next acknowledge duly
manhood taken by the Son.

(*Hymns Old & New* 133; *Hymns & Songs* 17)

Such attempts fall flat on their faces, but not in 'the speechless awe that dares not move' (*MHB* 325). But 'speechless awe' is surely a more appropriate response to so great a mystery than any controversy over whether the Spirit proceeds from both the Father and the Son, or only from the former, an issue which has divided the Eastern and Western Churches for centuries! Although awe and intellectual speculation are not mutually exclusive alternatives, in the case of the Trinity we can safely leave the latter to the experts, while we get on with our worshipping.

10

THE NATURAL WORLD

The revelation of God in nature is a popular theme among hymn-writers, but their treatment of it leaves something to be desired. Joseph Addison's 'The spacious firmament on high' (*HP* 339) exhibits the measured dignity and restraint of 18th-century classicism and has an undisputed place in any hymn book worthy of serious attention. All the same, its treatment of the natural world includes many concepts that were becoming dated even then. Some of the hymns that come to us from the 19th-century are of a much more questionable integrity in this respect. The vein is beginning to run out by the time we get to John Keble's 'There is a book (who runs may read)' (*HP* 340) with its second verse:

> The works of God above, below,
> Within us and around,
> Are pages in that book, to show
> How God himself is found.

This and other hymns are noticeably selective in their approach to the natural world. The most blatant example, 'Yes, God is good,' has survived as *HP* 363, but at the cost of the judicious dropping of one verse, beginning, 'Yes, God is good, all nature says' (*MHB* 968 v.5). '*All* nature?' is the inevitable question that demands an answer. Where then do predatory species ('Nature red in tooth and claw') and the devastation caused by earthquakes, tornadoes, drought and other such natural phenomena fit into the author's scheme of things? Whether at harvest time or otherwise, this line of thought has far-reaching implications and the theme of 'God in Nature' needs careful handling, together with a much more sophisticated understanding of 'providence'.

If what I have said so far seems much too negative, and even a threat to faith in a creator God, remember in the first place that an over-simplistic faith which ignores what is demonstrably the kind of world we live in has been a stumbling-block for many (and not just intellectuals), preventing them from taking Christianity seriously. Secondly, and more positively, we must avoid finding conflicts where they do not necessarily exist. The tension between 'science' and 'religion' has been real enough in recent history; but how far, and at what points, there has also been *conflict* is another question. The sciences among the different 'disciplines' of human enquiry have no more monopoly of truth than does Christianity among the religions of the world. In other words, scientific findings, valid in their own various fields, are not the whole of truth, which is multifaceted or multilayered. And religious truth (including the creation stories in Genesis) has more affinity with poetry and the arts than with the physical sciences or mathematics. (We might do better to talk of 'insights' and 'convictions', so long as we also make room for the concept of 'revelation' and the role of reason.)

In this age of IT, when information is often confused with knowledge, *HP* 345 also distinguishes between knowledge and wisdom (v.2), and then takes a further vital step in reminding us of our need for not only a 'new mind' but also a 'new heart' (v.3).

So far as the physical universe is concerned, though religion (and the arts) approach it from a point of view quite distinct from that of the physical sciences, conflict is inevitable only if we lose sight of a fundamental distinction. Scientists are concerned mainly with what may be called the 'immediate' causes, which can be identified and demonstrated through the senses; whereas the theologian is asking questions about 'ultimate' causes, which cannot necessarily be proved in such a way. This distinction was not, of course, the concern of the biblical writers, but it cannot be ignored in a scientific age.

Hymn-writers, because they are using the language of poetry not of the laboratory or observatory, are sometimes less than helpful here. A wellknown harvest hymn like 'We plough the fields and scatter . . .' (*HP* 352) focuses on God as the ultimate cause ('He sends the snow in winter, . . . He lights the evening star'), and echoes the language of the Bible in ignoring the immediate causes made known to us through the sciences. In doing so, it appears to make the dangerous claim that God controls every detail of the natural world ('The winds and waves obey him'). Such claims are clearly poetic rather than scientific; nevertheless, given the occurrence of natural disasters, they invite the charge that God is either capricious or indifferent in his handling of the creation. The same may be said of parts of *HP* 346, 'Hear us, O Lord, from heaven, thy dwelling-place', especially vv2 and 4, and of *HP* 66, 'Great is thy faithfulness', notably in v.2. Again, a hymn like 'All things bright and beautiful' (*HP* 330), however acceptable as nourishment for infants, becomes infantile if carried over into the spiritual diet of adults. Having said this, however, such hymns, used circumspectly, can serve as useful reminders of the variety and bountifulness of God's gifts in creation.

Although the author of *HP* 260 graduated in Physics, I cannot follow the logic of his opening lines:

> Jesus is Lord! Creation's voice proclaims it,
> For by his power each tree and flower was planned
> and made . . .
> Sun, moon and stars in heaven cry: Jesus is Lord!

'The power, majesty and creativity of God' maybe, but in what sense does the universe as known to us through modern astronomy and astrophysics proclaim 'Jesus as Lord'? Pratt Green much more pertinently warns us that

> Solar systems, void of meaning
> Freeze the spirit into stone,

so that we have a stark choice:

> Faith must die, or come full circle
> To its source in God alone. (*HP* 686 v.2)

HP 260's lurch back into the field of Natural Theology (in a double sense) is only partially redeemed by the shift of ground in vv2 and 3. Fortunately, the hymn may be seen as an exceptional case. Other recent hymn-writers, though still using the language of poetry, succeed in being more realistic and in some important respects bridge the gap between traditional belief and modern scientific knowledge. Hymns like Albert Bayly's 'Praise and thanksgiving' (*HP* 350), Brian Wren's 'Praise God for the harvest' (*HP* 351) and John Arlott's 'God, whose farm is all creation' (*HP* 344) emphasise our human responsibility as agents in God's continuing creativity. Two of Donald Hughes' hymns, *HP* 349 and 419, will repay attention in this context. Pratt Green, in 'God in his love for us lent us this planet' (*HP* 343), similarly makes quite explicit our responsibility for how natural resources are used and in v.2 of *HP* 342, 'For the fruits of his creation', challenges us to realise that we cannot sincerely thank God for material blessings without recognising and responding to the needs of others. A recent reworking of an old favourite fails lamentably at this point. 'We plough the fields with tractors' is liberally sprinkled with references to modern agricultural technology, but complacently ignores the desperate plight of subsistence farmers and their families in underdeveloped parts of the world. Ian Fraser does much better by echoing what Paul says (in Romans 8:19-22) about creation groaning and travailing in its bonds until the Lord creates a new heaven and earth (*HP* 347 v.4). In other words, the natural world *cannot* perfectly reflect its Creator so long as it is in what theology terms its 'fallen' state. Even hymn-writers cannot 'have it both ways'. There is plenty of food for thought here.

11

ENIGMAS

How often do we sing words without considering, or even questioning, their meaning, simply because they are familiar or are set to a good tune? It ought not to be just a light which 'surprises the Christian while he sings'. If, as I have urged throughout this book, we are thinking at all about the meaning of what we are singing, then from time to time an unexpected word or phrase will give us pause. Here are a few examples to begin with.

Him serve with *mirth* (*HP* 1 v.1, amended in some recent hymn books to 'fear'; and compare Luther's 'pious mirth' in *HP* 100 v.8)

... thy *various* praise (*HP* 12 v.1)

Hail the *heaven*-born Prince of Peace (cf. *HP* 106 v.3: 'begotten of the Father before all worlds'?)

Towering o'er the *wrecks* of time (*HP* 167 v.1)

Yet *cheerful* he/To suffering goes ... (*HP* 173 v.5)

Show me the truth *concealed*/Within thy word' (*HP* 467 v.3)

For us fights the *proper* Man (*HP* 661 v.2)

You will readily find further examples for yourself, if your devotional reading of the hymn book does not exclude thinking about the meaning.

Why does Wesley write of 'our *native* heaven' in *HP* 819 v.3? '*His* native heaven' in *HP* 197 is fine, but in what sense are *we* too indigenous? Could Wesley possibly be anticipating the rather fanciful idea of the soul's pre-existence in Wordsworth's 'Immortality Ode'? Similarly, what do you make of his 'Future and past subsisting now' (*HP* 662 v.3)? Is he playing with ideas of time similar to those of J W Dunne and J B Priestley's 'time plays'? Such anticipations seem highly unlikely; but in that case, what *did* he mean? Is there, perhaps, a definition of the real nature of faith and its relation to hope, embedded in the couplet

> Whate'er we hope, by faith we have,
> Future and past subsisting now?

What exactly had Whittier in mind when he wrote, 'And faith has still its Olivet,/And love its Galilee' (*HP* 392 v.5)? Or is that an unfair question to ask of a writer like Whittier?

What do you make of the idea of Zion *smiling* at all its foes (*HP* 817 v.1)? Is it like God's benevolent smile, as in *HP* 421 v.3? I rather fear that it may be a smile of smug superiority, almost a supercilious smirk (if you will forgive the alliteration); and if we are supposed to identify Zion with the Church, that raises some far-reaching issues.

Whom did Pratt Green mean by 'Christ's dissidents' in *HP* 556 v.2? Do we need more or fewer of them? And dare we claim (or admit) to being among them?

Such questions as these may be mere conundrums, unworthy of our own or our hearers' attention. But they may serve a very useful purpose if they take us back to fundamentals, and particularly to the Bible itself. If I am not clear what Wesley had in mind when he spoke of 'a threefold cord' in *HP* 773 v.2, I find myself going back to

Ecclesiastes 4:12, where 'a threefold cord is not quickly broken' and from there, maybe, forwards to John 14:21, where Jesus speaks of the intimate three-way relationship between himself, God the Father and ourselves.

Sometimes a word may be misleading and catch our attention because it is used in an obsolete way. 'I *want* the witness, Lord/That all I do is right' (*HP* 293 v.4) can sound like a cocksure demand unless we recognise that Wesley is using the word in its earlier meaning of 'need' (as in Richard Baxter's line, 'He wants not friends that hath thy love' (*HP* 495 v.1). In such cases we might have expected a judicious amendment by the editors, but perhaps they were wary of being accused of verbal 'ageism'?

* * * * *

There are important aspects of hymnody which have not even been touched on in passing in this book; e.g. some fine hymns on aspects of social concern by recent and contemporary authors. This is only partly for reasons of limited space. My intention from the outset has been descriptive, not prescriptive, in order to leave you with the task of discovering for yourself what the hymn book (whichever one you may use) has to offer you as a preacher. It does not matter if, where I have 'trailed my coat', you strongly disagree with me, so long as you are engaged on your own voyage of discovery.

FURTHER READING

Books on hymnody form a considerable library. Of those known to me, *Praises with Understanding* by A S Gregory (Epworth Press, 1936; revised edition, 1949) comes nearest to dealing with the topic of the present book. His article on 'The Preacher and his Hymn-book' in *The Preacher's Handbook, No 11* (1969) touches on, but nowhere addresses the topic itself. Any of Erik Routley's titles deserve your attention. The *Companion to Hymns & Psalms*, edited by Richard Watson and Kenneth Trickett (Methodist Publishing House, 1988) is the indispensable source of background information; its predecessors, on the *Methodist Hymn Book*, by John Telford (1906 and 1934) are still useful.

The definitive study of hymns as literature is J R Watson's *The English Hymn* (Clarendon Press, 1997), a magisterial but eminently readable volume. For the relationship between hymnody and theology, Teresa Berger's *Theology in Hymns* (Abingdon Press, 1989) is an academic study, limited by being focused on Wesley's 1780 *Collection of Hymns*. Brian Wren's *Praying Twice: The Music and Words of Congregational Song* (Westminster John Knox Press, 2000) includes a chapter on 'How Hymns Do Theology'.

Of the many books on Charles Wesley, F Luke Wiseman's Drew Lectures, *Charles Wesley* (Epworth Press, 1933) contains useful material, as does *Charles Wesley, Poet and Theologian* edited by S T Kimbrough (Abingdon Press, 1992). Bernard L Manning's classic studies in *The Hymns of Wesley and Watts* (Epworth Press, 1942) still makes lively and provocative reading.

For Wesley's theology, the two volumes by J Ernest Rattenbury, *The Evangelical Doctrines of Charles Wesley's Hymns* (Epworth Press, 1941) and *The Eucharistic Hymns of John and Charles Wesley* (Epworth Press, 1948) have not been superseded, even by more recent publications of the Charles Wesley Society.

Serving God and God's Creatures by Bernard Braley (2001) is much more than a biography of Fred Pratt Green.

But the most indispensable reading of all is the hymn book itself, whichever denomination happens to be its provenance.

INDEX OF FIRST LINES

B racketed figures indicate the numbering in *Hymns &
Psalms*, or in *The Methodist Hymn Book (MHB)* or
Hymns and Songs (HS).

ACKNOWLEDGEMENTS

Hymn texts by Fred Pratt Green, Fred Kaan, Alan Gaunt, Geoffrey Ainger, Doreen Newport and Brian Wren, by permission of Stainer & Bell Ltd.

Hymn texts by Bishop Timothy Dudley-Smith, by permission of the author.

Hymn texts by Michael Hewlett, Albert Bayly, J M Crum and G W Briggs, copyright Oxford University Press. Permission applied for.

Hymn texts by Bryn Rees, copyright Mrs Olwen Scott. Permission applied for.

'Jesus is Lord' David Mansell, copyright © 1982 Word's Spirit of Praise Music. Administered by CopyCare, PO Box 77, Hailsham BN27 3EF, UK, music@copycare.com Used by permission.

Hymn texts by Dr Ivor Jones, copyright the author. Permission applied for.

Page 51: lines from 'Advent' by John Betjeman, from *Collected Poems,* by permission of John Murray (Publishers) Ltd.